SpringerBriefs in Law

For further volumes:
http://www.springer.com/series/10164

Samantha Velluti

Reforming the Common European Asylum System - Legislative Developments and Judicial Activism of the European Courts

Springer

Samantha Velluti
College of Social Science
University of Lincoln
Lincoln
UK

ISSN 2192-855X ISSN 2192-8568 (electronic)
ISBN 978-3-642-40266-1 ISBN 978-3-642-40267-8 (eBook)
DOI 10.1007/978-3-642-40267-8
Springer Heidelberg New York Dordrecht London

Library of Congress Control Number: 2013946311

Printed on acid-free paper

Springer is part of Springer Science+Business Media (www.springer.com)

To Khaled

Preface

In June 2013, the amended European Union (EU) legislation on asylum was adopted after lengthy and complex negotiations. The recast "asylum package" represents a significant step forward in the further development of a Common European Asylum System (CEAS). Since the 1999 Tampere Conclusions, there has also been a series of landmark rulings of the European Court of Human Rights (ECtHR) and the European Court of Justice of the European Union (ECJ) which, combined with important constitutional and institutional changes introduced by the 2009 Treaty of Lisbon (ToL), has visibly changed the juridical and legal landscape in the area of asylum. Despite the progress made so far, the EU protection regime for refugees remains characterized by an underlying tension between a security paradigm and a human rights-based approach.

This timely volume provides fresh insights into legislative and judicial developments from a fundamental human rights perspective and responds to some of the contemporary challenges faced by the EU protection regime, with a particular focus on the rights of asylum-seekers.

Many of the ideas in this book are the end-result of collaborative research undertaken during my Visiting Professorship at the School of Law of the University of Cagliari in Italy in 2012. I am grateful to a number of colleagues, particularly Francesca Ippolito, with whom I had the opportunity to discuss at length a number of issues in relation to European asylum law, which I elaborate further in this book. I would also like to thank Sandra Wickenhauser at Springer for inviting me to contribute to the *Springer Briefs Series in Law* and for her enduring patience as completion was delayed by recent judicial and legislative developments at European level.

As an increasing number of people around the world are forced to flee their own country for fear of persecution, it is to them and to their heroic courage that this volume is dedicated.

July 2013 Samantha Velluti

Contents

Abstract

By drawing on a human rights-based and de-constructivist approach, this volume critically examines selected EU instruments aimed at protecting asylum-seekers. It starts by unpacking underlying tensions in the field of asylum which are rooted in classical understandings of national sovereignty best described as a "trinity of unity," namely, a unitary territory, a unitary force, and a unitary people. It then proceeds to the analysis of the recasting of selected EU asylum legislative instruments. The reform aims at introducing a significant shift in the nature of legislation by way of introducing mandatory obligations for the Member States together with the abolition of opt-out clauses and a full harmonization of both procedures and standards, which are also in line with the changes made by the ToL. On the basis of a comparative analysis of a series of key asylum cases, the volume also intends to critically examine the jurisprudence of the ECJ and the ECtHR *vis-à-vis* the European Convention of Human Rights (ECHR) and the EU Charter of Fundamental Rights and Freedoms (EU Charter).

The volume assesses whether the EU provides an adequate framework for protecting those seeking international protection from the (opposing) perspectives of *effectiveness* and *fairness*. It shows that, despite the newly adopted "second-generation" legislative acts which include changes aimed at ensuring a stronger level of protection for asylum-seekers, the reform process at European level does not adequately ensure an equal standard of protection across all Member States. It is posited that a way to adequately address the gaps and inconsistencies in extant EU asylum law, as well as its numerous problematic applications, is through principled implementation by the Member States, that is, in compliance with their international refugee and human rights obligations. Increasingly, both national and European Courts will be called to play a key monitoring function to ensure that standards and guarantees are met. In this context, the book suggests that further mutual engagement is required between the two European Courts and also outlines a proposal for the creation of an *ad hoc* EU asylum court.

Chapter 1
Introduction

The harmonization of national asylum laws and policies has primarily been conceived as a way of limiting the "secondary movement" of asylum-seekers, namely, the migration to that Member State where they could enjoy the most generous conditions and higher probability of recognition and legal status of refugee or other form of international protection. Hence, EU asylum law has mainly aimed at reducing the incentive to move and encourage asylum-seekers to remain in the first Member State in which they could seek protection. In recent years, as an increasing number of protection-seekers are coming to the EU to be granted some form of international protection, asylum can no longer be considered only in terms of management but also requires Member States to balance the achievement of efficiency in regulation with granting a set of basic rights for protection-seekers.

After more than 10 years of existence of CEAS, it is apposite to examine its key characteristics and, in this context, look at how it has influenced the nature of refugee protection. This volume, therefore, intends to critically examine key EU legislative instruments adopted in the field of asylum in order to evaluate the standard of protection afforded to asylum-seekers. The core of the book comprises an examination of the reform of existing legislative instruments as well as the case-law of the European Courts. In particular, this volume is set out to assess whether the EU provides an adequate framework for protecting those seeking international protection from the (opposing) perspectives of effectiveness and fairness and shows that, in spite of some changes ensuring a stronger level of protection of asylum-seekers, the reform fails to provide the basis for ensuring an equal standard of protection across all EU Member States. The volume does not aim to present a comprehensive analysis of all amendments made to existing legislation but seeks to examine the most significant changes addressing issues which are of a particularly problematic nature from a human rights perspective.

As the book will go on to show, the first phase of CEAS did not fully achieve the expected results of coherence, uniform interpretation and application of EU asylum law. To date, measures adopted in this field display so-called "common denominator" solutions and have given Member States ample discretion. The strong focus on securitization has eroded the distinction between refugee

S. Velluti, *Reforming the Common European Asylum System - Legislative Developments and Judicial Activism of the European Courts*, SpringerBriefs in Law, DOI: 10.1007/978-3-642-40267-8_1, © The Author(s) 2014

protection and migration control in asylum law and policy and has legitimized the pursuit of restrictive asylum policies, even though it fundamentally contradicts the international obligations of the EU and its Member States with international refugee and human rights law. To remedy to this state of affairs, the European Commission had originally proposed an ambitious recasting programme of the main legislative measures with the aim of changing the nature of the legislation. In particular, the original aim was to introduce mandatory obligations for the Member States together with the abolition of opt-out clauses and a full harmonization of both procedures and standards, which were also in line with the changes made by the ToL. However, in the course of the various negotiation stages most of the original drafts were significantly watered down especially by the amendments introduced by the Council of Ministers. For this reason as we shall see, the reform process has not resulted in a major overhaul of the EU asylum system.

The research is grounded in a human rights framework of inquiry, combined with a so-called "de-constructivist approach,"[1] which is used to unravel and critically examine the normative inconsistencies inherent in the EU's "securitized" approach to asylum. In particular, by drawing on the above methodology the book intends to unpack and evaluate the incongruence's engendered by the persistence in relying on a dichotomic approach to asylum, namely, one based on migration control/management and the officialised overarching objective of developing a CEAS truly founded on a rights-based approach to protection.

The rights-based approach embraced in this volume presupposes the existence of high quality EU asylum standards concerning in particular the conditions and criteria for determining asylum in the EU. The latter are reflected in the totality of procedural and substantive aspects of the standards governing the examination of asylum application, including the definition of beneficiaries of international protection.[2] The quality of these asylum standards can be meaningfully assessed by reference to three parameters,[3] which is here posited, a truly rights-based and refugee protection approach should aspire to:

- the likelihood that asylum applicants with comparable case background will receive *identical decisions* on their application in different Member States and consequently reduced secondary movements;

[1] I loosely rely on Derrida's approach to "deconstructivism." See Ref. [1]. As intended here, deconstruction involves a process made up of various stages. First, it is necessary to overturn a hierarchy of oppositions, both logical and axiological, which are at work in all the measures adopted in the context of CEAS. This will help to expose the way oppositions work and how meaning and values in the law are produced. Overturning is not intended as surpassing oppositions because they are structurally necessary in any given policy area. What it means is that they need to be subjected to thorough analysis and critique. In this way, the deconstructivist approach exposes the differences and eternal interplay between oppositions and helps to formulate new concepts and ideas in relation to the proper functioning of CEAS.

[2] See Ref. [2].

[3] Idem.

- the effective fulfilment across Member States of the *minimum standards* for the identification and protection of refugee and beneficiaries of subsidiary protection as well as reception standards for asylum-seekers and the procedural guarantees for asylum applications, laid down in EU asylum law;
- the *conformity* of the standards developed at EU level as well as implementing measures of the Member States with international refugee and human rights law.

The book draws extensively on official EU documentation as well as policy analysis, policy briefs and studies commissioned by the European Parliament and the European Commission. It also relies on position papers, reports and studies of the United Nations High Commissioner for Refugees (UNHCR), the European Council on Refugees and Exiles (ECRE) and selected non-governmental organizations (NGOs) such as Amnesty International (AI) and Statewatch, all of which closely monitor the developments in EU asylum law.

At the time of writing, CEAS has just entered into its second phase. The recast instruments represent a notable improvement but they still fall significantly short of full compliance with human rights obligations at international and European levels. The research findings of this volume point to a gap between the Union's commitment to the equal treatment and protection of the rights of asylum-seekers and the ability and willingness of the legislative institutions to make that commitment a reality. The legislative deadlock of the second phase of CEAS and the lack of intra-state trust and solidarity stifled progress in truly reforming the CEAS legal system. Against this backcloth, the analysis also intends to look at whether the European Courts with their respective rights-based policy agenda may overcome the limitations of existing EU asylum measures. In this context, the broader aim is to unravel the complex and evolving constitutional relationship between the EU and the overall system of the ECHR from the perspective of effective legal and judicial protection of fundamental rights for protection-seekers. In so doing, it concentrates largely on the ECHR and the EU Charter, which provide the basis for the jurisprudential analysis of asylum cases.

The book's main argument is that, in spite of the existence of certain limitations in both of the European Courts' jurisprudence, the role of the ECtHR and the ECJ as "regional refugee courts" is central to the effective guarantee of protection-seeker's fundamental rights, particularly in consideration of the piecemeal progress achieved through the reform of EU asylum legislation. By way of conclusion, it puts forward a tentative proposal for the creation of an *ad hoc* EU asylum court.

The book starts by examining key elements and characteristics of CEAS, both of a legal and non-legal nature, including a critique of the various conceptions of sovereignty which, is here posited, is an "essentially contested concept." This analysis is necessary to unfold some of the underlying tensions at the basis of CEAS, which explain the internal contradictions and inconsistencies and the gap between the EU's purported aim of promoting human rights and its security-based (or state-centred) approach to EU asylum law. The book then proceeds to a detailed critical analysis of the recast legislative instruments and illustrates the extent of substantive continuity with the first phase of CEAS and some positive changes from the perspective of protection-seekers' human rights, which in contrast constitute a break from past legislation. It subsequently evaluates the role of the European Courts and the nature of their relationship through jurisprudential analysis of key asylum cases and assesses the degree of reciprocal "osmosis" and the extent to which this mutual engagement may strengthen the protection of protection-seekers' rights within the EU asylum system. The concluding chapter to the book reflects on the legislative and judicial developments at European level examined in the previous chapters and looks at future prospects, including the possibility of setting up an *ad hoc* EU asylum court.

References

1. Legrand P (ed) (2009) Derrida and law. Ashgate, Farnham
2. Vedsted-Jansen J (2011) Conditions and criteria for determining asylum. In: Goudappel F, Raulus HS (eds) The future of asylum in the European Union, problems, proposals and human rights. Springer, The Hague, pp 139–140

Chapter 2
The Road to the Common European Asylum System: From Amsterdam to Lisbon and Beyond

2.1 Harmonization in Asylum and, Sovereignty as an Essentially Contested Concept

Any investigation of the EU asylum system and the creation of CEAS necessarily requires an analytical approach which unpacks its inherent tensions.[1] The multi-faceted conflict that underlies this area of EU law results from a rather uneasy cohabitation between intergovernmentalism and supranationalism and opposing objectives and discourses, namely, economic, efficiency/management and securitization goals versus human rights protection, fairness and justice.[2] The main challenges concerning the development of CEAS are only partially explained by the significant institutional and socio-economic differences between Member States. Key to a true understanding of the nature of the problems concerning asylum law and policies is their strong connection to ideas of the (primacy of) nation state, state sovereignty and state territory and borders which still play a central and determining role in the way Member States adopt measures in this field. What this tells us is that the nature and function of sovereignty is not a jaded question—far from it. This per se is seemingly a paradox in the current multi-polar system of policy-making and is counterintuitive to post-*Westphalian* societal

---

[1] The term "essentially contested concept" was first developed in the philosophy of language, see Ref. [1]; in the EU context, Besson defines it as 'a concept that not only expresses a normative standard and whose conceptions differ from one person to the other, but whose correct application is to create disagreement over its correct application or, in other words, over what the concept itself is.... It is [the concept's] nature not only to be contested, but to be contestable in [its] essence, so that not only [its] applications, but also [its] core elements or criteria are contestable;' see Ref. [2], at 6, available at http://eiop.or.at/eiop/texte/2004-015a.htm.

[2] It should be noted that these tensions extend to the whole AFSJ. Walker maintains that 'these fundamental value dilemmas are compounded by problems of political feasibility and implementation,' Ref. [3], at p. 25.

S. Velluti, *Reforming the Common European Asylum System - Legislative Developments and Judicial Activism of the European Courts*, SpringerBriefs in Law, DOI: 10.1007/978-3-642-40267-8_2, © The Author(s) 2014

structures. However, the importance placed on national sovereignty and statehood in the imagery of many Europeans constitutes a major obstacle to the objective of harmonization so strongly advocated at European level. And yet it matters.[3] Indeed, the refugee in international law occupies a legal space characterized by the principle of state sovereignty and the related principles of territorial supremacy and self-preservation.[4] In a similar vein, Diez[5] effectively describes the classical understanding of state sovereignty as a "trinity of unity," that is, a unitary territory, a unitary force and a unitary people. However, the emergence of new collective actors 'working within, across and above state lines' such as for example the EU has exposed the legal fiction of states' sole centrality in world politics.[6] Nevertheless, state borders are decisive in determining the status of refugee as it is only 'by crossing borders of sovereignty out of and into territories that they come into existence.'[7] It is precisely the border of state sovereignty that defines who is a refugee and thus enables individuals to be granted a status of international law entitlements and rights.[8] Hence, sovereignty is used to constitute societies but also to exclude from societies,[9] as embodied in the populist rhetoric of "We" versus the "Other."

One solution to this conundrum which may be more apposite to contemporary reality is to embrace what Kostakopoulou coins as a "floating" conception of sovereignty,[10] namely, one that rather than being premised on a dichotomic and fallacious thinking centred on retention/obliteration of sovereignty and the 'nihilism of its irrelevance and the equally unhelpful view of its ubiquity'[11] acknowledges that it is an open-ended concept which reflects how states themselves are subject to constant change in line with mutating global, regional and local exigencies and environments.[12] After all, as Krasner pithily puts it 'there may

---

[3] It matters because sovereignty and statehood are inextricably intertwined with identity, i.e. who we are, who is a friend, who is an enemy, and who is a stranger, and history, i.e. where we came from, how we became friends, how we got here, where we are, and where we are going in the future. It therefore provides the ontological and legitimating mooring of state intervention and regulation, see Ref. [4].

[4] See Ref. [5].

[5] See Ref. [6].

[6] See Ref. [7], at 136; for a polycentric conception of sovereignty which does not entail the demise of the state, see Ref. [8, 9].

[7] See Ref. [10].

[8] Ibidem, 414.

[9] See Ref. [11], at 1118.

[10] See Ref. [7], see footnote 6.

[11] I have borrowed this expression from French who examines similar issues in relation to the role of autonomy in international environmental law, see Ref. [12], at 263.

[12] By the same token, Besson refers to the necessary "reflexive" nature of sovereignty, in that its correct use requires a process of perpetual contestation of one's conceptions of the concept and therefore one's exercise of sovereignty; see Ref. [2], see footnote 1.

still be a modal tendency that pulls actors back to conventional sovereignty.'[13] In this context, the EU should no longer be viewed or portrayed as akin to a 'behemoth that is completely beyond the purview of the state,'[14] but rather as providing the locus for seamless interplay between different layers of policy-making, that is, shared sovereignty.[15] In this way we acknowledge the polycentric nature of the European polity as well as rejecting an etiolated version of the state.[16] Hence, the linear relations among rules are replaced by "circular or looped hierarchy" of law.[17] In this regard, Besson[18] refers to the cooperative nature of sovereignty which combined with the principle of subsidiarity ensures the allocation of power to those authorities that are best placed to ensure the protection of shared sovereign values and principles, such as the values of democracy and fundamental rights. Hence, cooperative sovereignty provides the normative framework for the development of a dynamic and reflexive form of constitutionalism. At this juncture, it is apposite to reproduce a passage from Krasner's article on sovereignty[19] for his acute and lucid analysis of state sovereignty in contemporary world politics:

> there is an inescapable tension in the sovereign state system. Rulers have often decided that they are better off violating Westphalian/Vattelian sovereignty than honouring it. In some cases, they have voluntarily ceded some of the autonomy of their own state. In other cases, leaders of powerful states have used coercion to compromise the autonomy of weaker states. The willingness of political leaders to violate Westphalian/Vattelian sovereignty is not surprising, given the absence of any final authoritative decision maker in the international system, and differences in power, interests, and values across states.

---

13 See Ref. [13], at 1078.

14 See French (2009), see footnote 11, at 267.

15 In a similar vein, "inclusive sovereignty" conceives power as an ability to maintain control over some decisive factors as well as influencing other agents (e.g. states) acting within a wider structure of governance such as for example global financial markets, international relations, and international organizations. Hence, inclusion and influence replace exclusion and autonomy. Additionally, the centres of such power do not necessarily coincide with traditional states. See e.g. Refs. [14, 15].

16 Sarooshi cogently maintains that the essentially contested nature of sovereignty remains the same whether we talk about national or international sovereignty. This unity of identity provides a compelling reason for international organizations' existence and, linked to that, a rationale for the construction of the normative framework that governs international organizations in the exercise of their delegated powers of government. This two-fold claim is substantiated by the fact that organizations provide a forum, transcendental to the state, where conceptions of sovereignty- and more specifically the content of sovereign values- can be contested on the international plane. This—according to Sarooshi- will be effectively achieved through the application of domestic administrative or public law principles to the definition of an international organization's normative framework of competence and use of delegated powers. See Sarooshi (2003–2004), see footnote 9.

17 A "looped hierarchy" is defined as an interaction among various levels of decision-making (within the hierarchical order) in which the highest level directs back to the lowest level and influences it while at the same time the highest level is determined itself by the lowest one, see Ref. [16].

18 See Besson (2004), see footnote 1.

19 Ibidem, 1084.

> Thus, *there is a hole in the whole of the sovereign state system.*[20] One of the system's basic norms, the expectation that each state will be autonomous—not subject to any higher authority within its own borders- has and will continue to be transgressed.

This form of "organised hypocrisy"[21] is not unsurprising. Brunsson argues that hypocrisy is a response to or a means to handle conflict, especially for and within organizations which are constantly the subject of and subjected to conflict.[22] While hypocrisy may be considered part of life and is thus inescapable in the international state system, the unwanted consequence is a legal system where it is not possible to adopt a coherent set of norms or, more generally, body of law.[23] In a nutshell: an unhappy and unstable situation where tension is inescapable.

The foregoing analysis of sovereignty, highlighting its multiple readings and essentially contested connotation, explains why in the EU asylum system law performs two main functions: an instrumental/control and a protective function. In particular, European asylum policies have come to incorporate means and elements of migration policy, in particular, migration control, which is mostly visible in the asylum procedure but is also highly present in the external aspects of asylum policy.[24] This close interconnection between offering protection to those seeking asylum and controlling immigration can also be seen in the language used in official documents such as the Stockholm Programme where there is reference to legally safe and efficient asylum procedures and at the same time the need to combat illegal migration.[25] The protective function of asylum law is in essence the *non-refoulement* principle as per Article 33 of the 1951 Geneva Convention and Article 3 ECHR.[26] In the context of EU asylum law it manifests itself in a two-fold way: one of reinforcement and one of mere acknowledgment.[27] The reinforcing effect can be seen in the right to asylum becoming a genuine residential right of territorial asylum within the Member States of the EU, namely, those who are granted refugee status or in need of subsidiary protection being given a residence permit.[28] The mere acknowledgment of existing legal obligations can be seen in

---

[20] Emphasis added.

[21] See Ref. [17].

[22] See Ref. [18], at pp. 201 and 203.

[23] See Ref. [17], see footnote 21, at 1084.

[24] Securitization theory is pivotal for the understanding of the restrictive trajectory characterizing EU asylum measures, see further Refs. [19–21].

[25] See Ref. [22].

[26] This principle is examined in further detail in the next section and in Chap. 4.

[27] See Ref. [23].

[28] E.g. Article 24 of the Qualification Directive; see also the Long-term Residents Directive which in the amended version extends long-term resident status to refugees and beneficiaries of subsidiary protection on a similar basis as other third country nationals legally living in the EU for more than five years. In particular, they will enjoy a number of rights such as the right to free movement within the EU, including the right to become a resident in another EU Member State, and under certain conditions, equality of treatment in relation to education, access to the labour market and social security benefits, see Council Directive 2003/109/EC of 25 November 2003

the limited application *ratione personae* of the Qualification Directive with the consequence that those who fall within the scope of the absolute prohibition of *refoulement* in Article 3 ECHR may not qualify for asylum under EU asylum law. This is not to say that substantial progress has not been achieved in many respects. However, as noted by Goodwin-Gill, there is a strong disjuncture between what is still often asserted to be a matter of sovereign state prerogative, and what is, as a matter of fact and law, structured and constrained by fundamental principles of protection.[29]

These fissures and fractures underlying the adoption and implementation of asylum law and policy have made the task of harmonization very difficult for the EU, at a time when the legitimacy of EU action is vigorously called into question and the 'stock exchange listings of the idea of Europe are down.'[30] The controversies surrounding the "ownership" of the policy priority-setting and legislative planning of the Stockholm Programme is a case in point.[31] The transition from the "classical" setting of the JHA institutional framework centred in the Council of Ministers to the extant post-Lisbon pluralist institutional landscape has not been a smooth one. The actual contours and implementation of the Stockholm Programme were subject to heated discussions between the Council and the Commission. Soon after its adoption, an Action Plan implementing the Stockholm Programme was published,[32] which was subject to severe criticism by the Council as it was deemed to go beyond the policy priorities envisaged by the Council's Stockholm Programme rather than using the latter as a frame of reference for programming.[33] The said Action Plan constitutes a departure from securitization towards the protection of fundamental rights and the values of human dignity and solidarity, providing a principled legislative agenda similar to the 1999 Tampere Programme.

As regards secondary legislation, the Qualification Directive well-illustrates the difficulties in reaching full harmonization in the field of asylum. It is the result of a long negotiation process among the Member States who have come to agree on a minimum common interpretation of the notions of refugee and persons in need of subsidiary protection. The Commission's proposals and the European Parliament's amendments in the consultation process stressed the need to ensure protection to

(Footnote 28 continued)
concerning the status of third-country nationals who are long-term residents, OJ L 16/44, 23 January 2004, as amended by the Directive 2011/51/EU of the European Parliament and of the Council of 11 May 2011 amending Council Directive 2003/109/EC to extend its scope to beneficiaries of international protection, OJ 132/1, 19 May 2011.

29 See Ref. [24], at p. 33.

30 See Ref. [25].

31 See Ref. [26].

32 See Ref. [27].

33 See Ref. [28].

asylum-seekers[34] whereas the Council focused largely on the prevention of abuse and even the limitation of asylum. The end result has been compromise also in view of the then unanimity requirement within the Council with a vague and unclear wording of several provisions such as the one contained in Article 15(c) of the Qualification Directive. The ECJ has been called to clarify the meaning and relationship of the two terms "individual threat" and "indiscriminate violence" as they appeared to be in conflict with one another.[35] The ruling of the Court not only clarified the relationship between the two notions but also strengthened the protective function of EU asylum law by providing that the interpretation given therein was compatible with the ECtHR case-law on Article 3 ECHR.

After having unravelled some of the most significant tensions underlying the process of Europeanization in the field of asylum—to a great extent centred around the essentially contested nature of the concept of sovereignty- the examination proceeds to an evaluation of key legal notions and principles in the international refugee regime and developments in the setting up of a fully-fledged CEAS. In so doing, it will seek to provide a preliminary assessment of the extent to which measures adopted within the EU meet the purported goals established at European level and whether they may be conflated with an EU asylum policy and, in this context, the standard of protection afforded to asylum-seekers.[36] What this first analysis will show is that CEAS is influencing and moulding the meaning of sovereignty in unexpected ways and, changing the way in which governance operates in respect of individuals.[37]

2.1.1 *Refugee Protection and International Refugee Law in the EU*

The legal duty of EU Member States to offer protection to refugees can be found in a combination of refugee, human rights and humanitarian law. The Geneva

---

[34] See European Commission, Proposal for a Council Directive on minimum standards for the qualification and status of third country nationals and stateless persons as refugees or as persons who otherwise need international protection, COM (2001) 510 final; European Parliament, Committee on Citizens' Freedoms and Rights, Justice and Home Affairs, Committee Report on the proposal for a Council Directive on minimum standards for the qualification and status of third country nationals and stateless persons as refugees or as persons who otherwise need international protection, COM (2001) 510—C5-0573/2001—2001/0207 (CNS)), PE 319.971/A5-0333/2002.

[35] See Case C-465/07, *Elgafaji v Staatssecretaris van Justitie*, [2009] ECR I-921, examined further below in Chap. 4.

[36] The critical appraisal will comprise two types of goals: *procedural goals*, namely, those concerning "who" adopts/implements and "how" asylum policies are or should be adopted and implemented; and, *substantive goals* concerning what rights constitute the "public good" to which asylum-seekers have access.

[37] See Ref. [29].

Convention constitutes the centrepiece of international refugee protection[38] by providing a definition of refugee[39] and the most comprehensive codification of refugees' rights at international level. The Convention is both a status and rights-based instrument and is underpinned by a number of fundamental principles, such as non-discrimination (Article 3) and *non-refoulement* (Article 33). Further, it lays down basic minimum standards for the treatment of refugees, without prejudice to states granting more favourable treatment. Article 78 TFEU provides that the CEAS must be in accordance with this Convention and 'other relevant Treaties.'[40] Under this provision, International treaties are those that are binding upon all Member States, unless they qualify wholly or in part as customary international law binding upon Member States irrespective of a ratification of the treaty.[41] Member States remain liable under international human rights law, if they fail to safeguard against *refoulement*. This principle is buttressed by general rules of international law such as the principle of good faith.[42] Moreover, as signatories of the Vienna Convention on the Law of Treaties (the Vienna Convention) Member States are bound by the rule of *pacta sunt servanda* which requires them to abide by all international agreements to which they are party.[43] This means that Member States' commitments to international law have primacy over any EU-level legislation. Furthermore, the EU is obliged not to impede Member States' obligations

[38] Other important international legal instruments for the protection of asylum-seekers and refugees are those human rights treaties belonging to the United Nations (UN) family to which most European countries are parties to, namely, the 1966 International Covenant on Civil and Political Rights (ICCPR) (which provides similar protection guarantees as the ECHR), the 1948 Universal Declaration of Human Rights (UDHR), the 1979 Convention on the Elimination of All Forms of Discrimination against Women (CEDAW), the 1965 Convention on the Elimination of All Forms of Racial Discrimination (CERD), the 1984 United Nations Convention against Torture and other Cruel, Inhuman or Degrading Treatment or Punishment (UNCAT), the 1989 Convention on the Rights of the Child (CRC) and the 2006 Convention on the Rights of Persons with Disabilities (CRPD).

[39] See Article 1A.

[40] Such treaties are not explicitly mentioned in Article 78 TFEU. However, there is general consensus that they may comprise the UN Convention on the Rights of the Child of 1989, the Convention against Torture and Other Cruel, Inhuman or Degrading Treatment or Punishment of 10 December 1984 and the International Covenant on Civil and Political Rights of 16 January 1966.

[41] See Ref. [30], at p. 10.

[42] The General Rule of Interpretation in Article 31(1) of the Vienna Convention states that treaties 'shall be interpreted in good faith in accordance with the ordinary meaning given to the terms of the treaty in their context and in light of its object and purpose.' See Ref. [5], see footnote 1, at p. 390.

[43] See Article 26 of the Vienna Convention on the Law of Treaties (1155 UNTS 331; entered into force 27 January 1980), which provides that: 'Pacta sunt servanda- Every treaty in force is binding upon the parties to it and must be performed by them in good faith.'

under international law.[44] Compliance with EU law, therefore, may be said to be secondary to the fulfilment of international obligations. Consequently, the EU and its Member States remain legally bound to comply with the Refugee Convention, as well as the other international human rights treaties to which they are party, prior to any other instrument which is to be applied at EU level. Indeed, the implementation of EU Directives cannot be equated to automatic compliance with Member States' international obligations.[45] In addition, the Refugee Convention and the 1967 Protocol are a source of general principles of EU law, as they have been ratified by all Member States.[46] The Geneva Convention does not contain any provisions on procedures nor does it establish an individual right to be granted asylum. However, under the principle of good faith state parties to the Convention are required to institute a formal procedure which allows for a fair and effective procedure in order to determine who is entitled to the guarantees of the Convention. This view has found general consensus, particularly with regard to the principle of *non-refoulement* in Article 33 of the Geneva Convention. Under international law, states are responsible for examining asylum claims made in their jurisdiction.[47] According to Goodwin-Gill and McAdam, asylum-seekers have a right to full protection until their refugee status has been determined[48] and failure to recognise genuine refugees as such is a violation of international law.[49] At the same time—in the absence of procedural rules- the terms "fair" and "efficient" are subject to discretion and a wide margin of appreciation which has meant that for years contracting states have used different techniques and concepts for the examination of claims for international protection. Hence, before the adoption of minimum standards it was within Member States' full discretion to establish procedural rules on a proper asylum procedure.[50]

[44] Article 27 of the Vienna Convention provides that international law has primacy over domestic law: 'a state may not invoke the provisions of its internal law as justification for its failure to perform a treaty.'

[45] See Ref. [30], see footnote 41, at p. 12.

[46] See Ref. [31].

[47] See Article 2(1) of the ICCPR which provides that rights are applicable to 'all individuals within [a State's] territory and subject to its jurisdiction.'

[48] See Ref. [5], see footnote 4, at p. 234.

[49] Ibidem, at p. 412.

[50] In the past various international organizations and non-governmental agencies have developed general principles on asylum procedures, e.g. see Ref. [32–34]. However, such recommendations whilst of high value do not constitute an authoritative source of interpretation.

2.1.2 *The Treaty of Amsterdam, EU Competence and Asylum*

The ToA had a major if not seismic impact on the solipsistic existence of the Member States and the lives of their citizens. It appeared on the EU scene as a *Deus ex Machina* sanctioning an almost irreversible move[51] to shared competence and qualified majority voting (QMV) and signalling a rupture and break from the past in many key areas previously the jealous preserve of the Member States.[52] The ToA 'did for the Union in the field of migration what Maastricht had done for Europe, moving the asylum and refugee agenda from the Third pillar, and state-to-state decision-making, to the First Pillar, introducing Community legislative competence in the field.'[53] The partial Communitarization of the then Third Pillar paved the way to new important dynamics in the field of justice and home affairs (JHA). There was a general, albeit reluctant, acknowledgment that many common problems had a global as well as a regional dimension to them with all the difficulties and pitfalls that this two-sided dimension entails, asylum being a case in point.[54]

In the field of asylum the transfer of legislative competence to the EU[55] paved the way to a process of Europeanization of Member States' practices and legislation[56] initiating what Staffans defines as the 'process of voluntary internationalization of asylum law.'[57] The use of the term "voluntary" could be easily dismissed as a contradiction in terms in the context of EU law or, more simply, as being either out of place or misplaced. As the EU has evolved into a *sui generis* international legal and political entity "voluntary" seems to have changed alongside it acquiring a distinct meaning in comparison with that of autonomy and

[51] With the term "irreversible" I am referring to the fact that, despite some rebellious and die hard Member States and notwithstanding the existence of differentiated integration mechanisms, the EU will survive its very own self only through a departure from atomistic systems of regulation to a pluralistic one largely based on shared competence.

[52] Kostakopoulou argues that the ToA changes in the field of JHA marked the beginning of a third phase in the development of a European immigration policy and constituted a break in the intergovernmental methodology. By extension, the same consideration can be made in relation to EU asylum measures; see Ref. [35], at 182.

[53] See Ref. [36], at p. 30.

[54] What is being said is not meant to underestimate the coming into existence of other forms of competence which were given a more formal recognition around the same time such as, for example, coordination (see e.g. Articles 5 and 6 TFEU). It is however the author's view that shared competence constitutes a durable and thus preferable form of competence if the EU is to carry on existing in the foreseeable future.

[55] For an account of the historical background of the legislative and policy developments in asylum, see Ref. [37–45], in this chapter and Chap. 5.

[56] It should be noted that Title IV EC inserted by ToA did not establish 'an area of freedom, security and justice', but rather introduced mechanisms and a timetable for the progressive establishment of such an area.

[57] See Ref. [46].

independence.[58] Self-will is a state's motive force: it impels a state *from within*, whereas abeyance to a supranational body of law compels a state *from without*. Clearly, in the EU context "voluntary" cannot be equated to a state's self-will as, arguably, there is a strong degree of coerciveness embedded in EU law. The foregoing explains, on the one side, why "voluntary" within the EU system does not bode well with the "classical" notion of state sovereignty[59] and, on the other, the tensions underlying EU asylum law and policy measures.

In 1999 a programme of full scale harmonization was put in place, encompassing legislative, policy and judicial procedural harmonization.[60] The Tampere Conclusions firmly included the creation of a 'common European asylum system'—and linked to that a common asylum procedure (CEAP), a uniform status for recognized refugees and persons benefiting from subsidiary protection- in the EU top agenda based on the full and inclusive application of the Geneva Convention.[61] In so doing, the European Council emphasized the importance the Union and Member States attach to absolute respect of the right to seek asylum. The common EU asylum regime was to be a constituent part of the newly created AFSJ. Harmonized policies would enable the EU to become a "single asylum space" with the broader aim of ensuring a consistent asylum process and equivalent levels of protection throughout the Union. According to the Tampere Conclusions the future CEAS should include, in the short term, a clear and workable determination of the state responsible for the examination of an asylum application, common standards for a fair and efficient asylum procedure, common minimum conditions of reception of asylum-seekers, and the approximation of rules on the recognition and content of the refugee status. It should also be completed with measures on subsidiary forms of protection offering an appropriate status to any person in need of such protection.

---

[58] Beyond any philosophical delving on the meaning of "voluntary"—certainly not the intention here- it should be noted that EU asylum law exemplifies the extant tensions in many areas of EU law, namely the inherent ambiguity between what was initially designed to be a body of law premised largely upon state voluntarism and what has ultimately become a supranational system of law. From this perspective, the tensions within EU asylum law are arguably innate within a state-based system of law.

[59] Classical approaches espouse a monistic conception of sovereignty, which is seen as a key organizing principle and source of legitimation for state action. E.g. [47–50]. In the context of international law, De Vattel, developed the theory of a voluntary law of nations and its necessary corollary of states' self-interestedness, which was grounded in the notion of the state as a compound moral person that had a duty under natural law to perfect itself. According to this theory, states committed themselves to international agreements with the proviso that these pledges were only binding insofar as states continued to view them as such. For de Vattel a state had an understanding and a will (the latter intertwined and united by the pacts of a number of men, and thus the will of all), of which it made use for the conduct of its affairs, and was capable of obligations and rights. See Ref. [51].

[60] See Refs. [52, 53]. For an analysis of the measures and instruments employed in the context of the Europeanization of asylum, see Ref. [54].

[61] See Presidency Conclusions of the Tampere European Council 15–16 October 1999, pp. 3–4; see also Ref. [55].

The goals included in the Tampere Conclusions constitute in the first place *meta-systemic principles* in that they lay out Fullerian rule of law requirements[62] which must necessarily underscore also a second category of meta-principles,[63] namely, *meta-constitutional principles* which are set out to help identifying the constitutive principles, values and procedures to be employed at both European and domestic levels as well as defining the scope and objectives of the constitutive procedures through substantive criteria of justice and rights.

Various reasons explain the decision by the Member States to go ahead with the creation of CEAS. Above all, the conviction that a well-functioning CEAS contributes to improving the image and perception of the EU on the international plane, particularly *vis-à-vis* the protection of human rights. A fully-fledged CEAS with a common procedure and a uniform asylum status would also significantly reduce secondary movements of asylum-seekers across the EU[64] and consequently reduce the costs deriving from sending and receiving individuals between Member States.[65] Linked to this, a centralized system with harmonized standards and procedures would alleviate Member States from carrying out some of the more complex and difficult administrative tasks such as for example fact-finding and retrieving information from countries of origin. The CEAP is yet to be established although it is envisaged that it will encompass common procedures, joint processing and shared technical support-functions, such as databases and sources of country of origin-information. Additionally, persons granted asylum status through the CEAP will receive the same benefits and rights throughout the union, as part of the uniform status that is part of the CEAS.

However, as Vedsted-Hansen[66] aptly observes, while the general spirit of the Tampere Conclusions could be considered quite ambitious and protection-oriented, the inclusion of the "fair and efficient" standard reflects a balance between the individual and Member States' interests. In addition, "fairness" is a sufficiently flexible notion which can be moulded to meet, where necessary, the potentially strong demand for efficiency.[67] The European Council also agreed that this process of harmonization would be divided into two main phases: a first phase (ending in

---

[62] See Ref. [56].

[63] In legal theory the term 'meta-principle' refers to an umbrella principle from which other principles derive as corollaries or as natural consequences; see e.g. Ref. [57, 58].

[64] The Dublin Regulation allocating responsibility for the examination of asylum applications presupposes that all EU Member States comply with certain standards of protection in order to avoid arbitrary differences of treatment, and to reduce the risk of secondary movements between Member States, see Council Regulation No. 343/2003 of 18 February 2003. Similarly, this objective has been expressly stated in the Preambles of all the first generation asylum Directives, e.g. see Recital 9 of the Temporary Protection Directive (Directive 2001/55 of 20 July 2001), Recital 8 of the Reception Conditions Directive (Directive 2003/9 of 27 January 2003), Recital 7 of the Qualification Directive (Directive 2004/83 of 29 April 2004) and Recital 6 of the original Asylum Procedures Directive (Directive 2005/85 of 1 December 2005).

[65] See Ref. [59].

[66] See Ref. [60], at p. 255.

[67] Idem.

2004) involving the adoption of harmonizing Directives and Regulations on the basis of common minimum standards,[68] and a second phase (ending in 2010), focusing on the practical development and integration of asylum procedures in the EU with a view to establishing a single asylum procedure and a uniform status of the persons granted protection throughout the Union. The deadlines for completing these stages of the CEAS were not met because of the delay in reaching an agreement among Member States. Two multiannual programmes setting out the policy priorities in more detail were adopted in subsequent years: the 2004 Hague Programme, which prompted the institutions to complete the first set of asylum legislation and provided for the establishment of a common asylum procedure[69] as a priority objective, and the 2009 Stockholm multiannual programme, which called for the completion of a truly common CEAS.

A comparison between the goals set out by the Hague Programme and the Tampere Conclusions reveals some significant differences as regards the legal protection of individuals.[70] In particular, the Hague Programme[71] in referring to a "European Area for Justice," focused on civil and criminal law whereas in the Tampere conclusions the principle 'justice accessible to all' was explicitly extended to the field of migration law and included persons both in and outside the EU territory. In addition, the Hague Programme focused primarily on the protection of the rights and freedoms of citizens without specifying whether this included EU citizens only or extended also to third country nationals (TCNs), and if so, whether it included legally resident TCNs, or also irregular migrants. The 2009 Stockholm programme[72] gave emphasis first of all to the procedural rights of EU citizens, particularly since the changes introduced by the ToL. However, it also explicitly referred to the interests and needs of the citizens and 'other persons for whom the EU has a responsibility.' Interestingly, the European Council already acknowledged at the time that the key challenge would be to balance the need to ensure the respect for fundamental rights and freedoms and integrity with the objective of guaranteeing security in Europe. Under the heading of "A Europe of law and justice," it was explicitly stated that priority should be given to mechanisms 'that facilitate access to justice, so that people can enforce their rights

[68] The fact that the Asylum Procedures Directive was only adopted beyond the May 2004 deadline because of strong disagreement on various controversial issues confirms what has been said above about the great difficulty in achieving harmonization in the field of asylum, see Directive 2005/85/EC of 1 December 2005 on minimum standards on procedures in Member States for granting and withdrawing refugee status, OJ L 326/13.

[69] The reference to a common asylum procedure in the 2004 Hague Programme in many aspects recalled the "single procedure" as defined by the Commission during the first period of implementation of the implementation of the Tampere Programme, see European Commission Communication, *Towards a Common Asylum Procedure and a Uniform Status, Valid Throughout the Union* COM (2000) 755 final, pp. 8–9.

[70] See Ref. [61], at p. 378.

[71] See Ref. [62].

[72] See Ref. [63].

throughout the Union.' The language of justice and human rights used in the Stockholm Programme, therefore, very much resembles that used in the Tampere Conclusions. In addition, it recognized that there were still significant differences between national provisions and their application, and that a higher degree of harmonization would be achieved through the establishment of the CEAS which remained a key policy objective. Moreover, it not only re-emphasized the full and inclusive application of the Geneva Convention but it also proposed that the EU 'should seek accession to the 1951 Geneva Convention and its 1967 Protocol.' The latter would have the benefit of establishing a direct link between the Union institutions and the international refugee protection system, as well as strengthening institutional ties between the UNHCR and the EU ensuring compliance with the Convention at all levels of EU intervention in asylum.[73]

However, the Stockholm Programme did not provide specific policy directions for the second generation of EU asylum Directives and only held that both common rules and a better and more coherent application of them should prevent or reduce secondary movements within the EU and increase mutual trust between Member States. The Council and the European Parliament were called to adopt legislation to help establish a common asylum procedure and a uniform status in accordance with Article 78 TFEU by 2012.[74] Apart from the long-term objective of *common* asylum procedures across the EU though, no specific guidance was provided in relation to the nature and degree of harmonization to be achieved.

During the first phase (1999–2005) of the establishment of the CEAS a series of important legislative measures harmonizing common minimum standards in the area of asylum were adopted such as the Directive on Temporary Protection, Directive on Reception Conditions for asylum-seekers, the Directive on the Qualification for becoming a refugee or a beneficiary of subsidiary protection status, the Asylum Procedure Directive, the Dublin Regulation II and the Returns Directive.[75] The first phase instruments were unanimously agreed by the Council and the European Parliament's role was limited to consultation. The Directives as such—because of the then unanimity voting procedure within the Council of

[73] This is discussed in further detail in Chap. 5.

[74] See also Refs. [64, 65].

[75] See Council Directive 2001/55/EC of 20 July 2001 on minimum standards for giving temporary protection in the event of a mass influx of displaced persons and on measures promoting a balance of efforts between Member States in receiving such persons and bearing the consequences thereof, OJ L 212/12, 7 August 2001; Council Directive 2004/83/EC of 29 April 2004 on minimum standards for the qualification and status of third country nationals or stateless persons as refugees or as persons who otherwise need international protection and the content of the protection granted, OJ L 304/12, 30 September 2004; Council Directive 2005/85/EC of 1 December 2005 on minimum standards on procedures in Member States for granting and withdrawing refugee status, OJ L 326/, 13Dec. 2005; Council Regulation No 343/2003 of 18 February 2003 establishing the criteria and mechanisms for determining the Member State responsible for examining an asylum application lodged in one of the Member States by a third-country national, OJ L 50/1, 25 Feb. 2003; Council Directive 2008/115/EC on common standards and procedures for illegally staying third country nationals, OJ L 348/98 of 16 December 2008.

Ministers- constitute a true expression of Member States' concerns and objectives centred around securitization, namely, to find the "lowest common denominator" with respect to the standards of protection rather than the protection of refugees per se.[76] The unanimity requirement seriously impaired the decision-making process facilitating policies of deterrence.[77] It allowed Member States to continue to be the dominant actors in policy-making and ensured that harmonization would remain conceived within a restrictive logic of refugee protection.[78] Since the 1980s, policies of deflection have been directed at all migrants with no distinction between immigrants and forced migrants and asylum-seekers have become a synonym for all different forms of migrants.[79] This practice has substantially weakened the ideological value of asylum and ultimately threatens to undermine the global institution of refugee protection.[80]

During the second phase of the CEAS the European Commission reviewed existing asylum legislation and submitted various recast proposals.[81] These proposals aimed at introducing a significant shift in the nature of legislation by way of introducing mandatory obligations for the Member States together with the abolition of opt-out clauses and a full harmonization of both procedures and standards which were also in line with the changes made by the Lisbon Treaty.[82] As will be shown in the next Chapter, this rationale has been significantly watered down and optional harmonization characterizes all the recast instruments.

Article 78 TFEU requires compliance with the principle of *non-refoulement* in the creation of the CEAS. Arguably, this obligation may be said to be stronger than that contained in the 1951 Convention in order to ensure that any act that prevents access to European territories and does not allow them to obtain the necessary protection is prohibited.[83] Moreover, a new agency, the European Asylum Support Office (EASO),[84] has been set up in 2010 as part of the EU's effort to develop a

---

[76] See Ref. [66]; see also Ref. [67]

[77] See Ref. [68].

[78] See Ref. [69], at 38.

[79] See Ref. [70, 71].

[80] See Ref. [72].

[81] A first package of proposals included: Ref. [73–75]. A second package included: Ref. [76, 77]. See Ref. [78], for detailed analysis and commentary. The recast process is largely the focus of Chap. 3 of this volume.

[82] See European Commission Communication to the European Parliament and the Council, *An area of Freedom, Security and Justice serving the citizen,* COM (2009) 262 final, 10 June 2009.

[83] E.g., see Ref. [79], at 695; for a view according to which restrictive national measures are likely to be countered by arguments founded on the peremptory norm of *non-refoulement* see Ref. [80, 81].

[84] See Ref. [82]. The agency, which is based in Malta and became fully operational in June 2011, plays a key role in the concrete development of CEAS and asylum protection. It has been established with the aim of enhancing practical cooperation on asylum matters. In particular, EASO acts as a centre of expertise on asylum and also provides support to Member States whose asylum and reception systems are under particular pressure. First, it provides training on asylum procedures and processes, such as assistance in screening by asylum support teams, development

truly comprehensive asylum policy and, specifically, to improve the practical cooperation between national authorities involved in asylum operations to better implement EU asylum measures. The EASO Regulation incorporates some key mechanisms for mainstreaming fundamental rights considerations into the design and operation of the agency. First, EASO's Regulation makes an explicit acknowledgement of the EU Charter.[85] It is also noteworthy that the European Parliament is involved in the appointment of the Executive Director of the agency. Article 30(1) of the EASO Regulation states that before appointment by the management board, the candidate selected shall be invited to make a statement before the European Parliament. The Parliament then delivers an opinion on the candidate and the management board is required to inform the Parliament of the manner in which that opinion is taken into account. Secondly, and significantly, the EASO Regulation allocates a specific role to the UNHCR.[86] The agency has to act in close cooperation with the UNHCR as well as other relevant international organizations. In particular, the UNHCR sits as a non-voting member of the management board, participates in the expert working groups and is a member of the EASO Consultative Forum. Further, EASO is also mandated to cooperate with the Fundamental Rights Agency (FRA). Notwithstanding the integration of mechanisms aimed at safeguarding fundamental rights, some concerns have been raised in relation to EASO's mandate and regulatory tasks and the implications *vis-à-vis* fundamental rights.[87] In Levy's view, EASO follows in the tradition of supranational intergovernmentalism and he is doubtful as to whether this agency will be able to effectively ensure the implementation or strengthening of asylum capacity building.[88] More specifically, concerns have been raised in relation to EASO's creation and dissemination of country of origin information and the potential implications this activity could have on the rights to asylum and protection against collective expulsion and *refoulement* as per Articles 18 and 19 of the EU Charter.[89] In addition, AI has highlighted, in view of EASO's future working agreements with third countries, the potential conflict between

(Footnote 84 continued)
of technical documents, provision of country of origin information reports and training of national experts, including members of the judiciary. It can also provide tailor-made (technical) assistance, such as capacity building and relocation, as well as emergency support in the form of solidarity to help repair or rebuild asylum or reception systems (e.g. Article 80 TFEU). In the longer-term the agency could have a significant influence on Member States' asylum measures, including (indirectly) individual asylum decisions.

[85] See Recital 31, which provides that: 'This Regulation respects fundamental rights and observes the principles recognised in particular by the Charter of Fundamental Rights of the European Union and should be applied in accordance with the right to asylum recognised in Article 18 of the Charter.'

[86] See Recitals 10, 17, Articles 2(5), 5, 9(1), 12(2), 25(4), 27(1), 29(2) subpara. 3, 32(2), 50, 51(3) subpara. 2.

[87] See Ref. [83].

[88] See Ref. [84], at 116.

[89] See Ref. [83], see footnote 87, at p. 76.

maintaining good working relations with the countries from which the asylum-seekers originate, and providing credible and impartial country-of-origin information.[90] Appropriate safeguards must be in place to ensure that country of origin information is accurate, based on independent sources of expertise and free from political influence. In addition, safeguards must ensure that country of origin information does not jeopardise or substitute fair procedures by national authorities in the determination of asylum procedures in accordance with EU law.

More generally, there is a fear that should the EASO become an increasingly migration control agency it may end up undermining some the precepts of the rule of law. These are not new concerns. Previous studies have indicated that migration control agencies and law and order officials favour the vertical dimension of policymaking, as it allows them to sidestep the judicial constraints of the domestic level, and at the same time, avoid input from EU institutions.[91] The dominance of security experts has led to the strengthening of 'executive authority at the expense of legislative or judicial oversight,' which, in turn, has made the agenda of security and control easier to advance.[92]

In spite of some progress, the overall picture looks gloomy for asylum-seekers in the EU. Disappointingly, the creation of a supranational asylum regime seems to be leading to a significant erosion of refugees' rights in the EU.[93] Or to put it differently, *in spite of* institutional changes in the EU, asylum policymaking has not been fully communitarized; instead the policy process has been characterized by a hybrid form of intergovernmental supranationalism, which has facilitated the development of securitized asylum policies.[94] Despite officially proclaimed commitments to the protection of asylum-seekers, the harmonization of asylum policies has lowered protection standards in many Member States.[95] Moreover, the adoption of the asylum Directives has been coupled with a significant increase in admission controls at the external frontier of the Union, as well as stringent visa requirements and travel restrictions.[96] These external border controls prevent asylum-seekers from gaining access to the EU's asylum system in order to claim international protection. Arguably, the EU's inability to provide human guarantees for refugees is a significant challenge to its global role in the field of human rights.

---

90 See Ref. [85].

91 See Ref. [86], at p. 164.

92 See Ref. [87], at p. 203.

93 For example, the Council has completely rejected the proposal to establish a mechanism for the possible suspension of the Dublin rules in cases of Member State's deficiencies and thus suspension of transfers, agreeing instead to insert rules on an 'early warning mechanism' which in practice would not affect the application of the Regulation; this is examined further below, infra, Chap. 3.

94 See Ref. [84], see footnote 88, at 108.

95 See Nicholson, see footnote 77, at p. 525.

96 See e.g. Refs. [88, 89] for academic commentary see Ref. [90].

2.1.3 *Key Changes to the Legal Framework since the Treaty of Lisbon*

The ToL was the 'by product of the process of "structured reflection" on the future of Europe that followed the rejection of the Constitutional Treaty.'[97] One of the most significant changes introduced by this Treaty has been the unification of the institutional framework of the different policy components of the AFSJ under new Title V with QMV in the Council and the ordinary legislative procedure becoming the norm and a full use of "Community" legislative acts giving rise to justiciable rights before national courts.[98] The abandonment of the requirement of unanimity within the area of asylum and immigration measures[99] is aimed at facilitating the recast of the asylum Directives. There has also been a shift in language from the EC Treaty to the TFEU from "qualification" for international protection under the EC Treaty (which lead to the Qualification Directive) to "status of asylum." The change better reflects the wording of the Refugee Convention and it indicates that EU asylum law is coextensive with international refugee law.[100] However, strong national interests remain and are reflected in Member States' negotiation positions.[101] This is exemplified by the difficulty in adopting the recast of most asylum Directives.[102] The formal change of legislative competences and procedures to date have not been able to ensure more effective harmonization and better compliance with the obligations under international human rights and refugee law and they have therefore made little difference in reality.[103]

One of the key innovative features introduced by the ToL includes the full jurisdiction of the ECJ. In particular, the ToL repealed former Article 68 EC, which limited the right to request preliminary rulings to courts of last instance—meaning that all national courts, and not merely the highest judicial bodies, would be able to make requests in relation to asylum, immigration and visa issues. The number of preliminary rulings that have been requested since has greatly increased as well as the variety in the range and subject matter of questions put forward to

[97] See Ref. [91], at 154.

[98] Idem.

[99] It was former Article 67(5) EC which introduced QMV in order to enable the amendment of the first generation of asylum Directives.

[100] See Ref. [92].

[101] The European Parliament and the Council managed to agree on the revision of the Qualification Directive, which was then officially adopted in November 2011. However, the Council had difficulty agreeing on how to revise the recast of the other Directives with the result that the Commission had to amend proposals for the Directives on reception conditions and asylum procedures, in order to restart discussions.

[102] See further in Chap. 3.

[103] The amended proposals reproduced in the adopted Recast Directives contain mostly cosmetic changes and do not require Member States to raise their standards very much. Arguably, the second phase of the CEAS resembles the first phase; see Ref. [93]; see Refs. [94, 95].

the Court.[104] Already under the circumscribed Article 68 EC procedure formerly in place, various national courts of final instance were making references to the ECJ.[105] The preliminary rulings issued so far have considerably assisted national courts and tribunals in applying EU asylum law.[106] At present, there are considerable divergences between Member States as to the interpretation and implementation of EU asylum law.[107] For example, there has been disagreement between some national courts in relation to Article 15(c) of the Qualification Directive[108] as to the role of international humanitarian law as being a valid legal tool for interpreting key terms such as that of "indiscriminate violence." In particular, in *QD & AH (Iraq)* the English Court of Appeal held that international humanitarian law cannot to be used as an interpretive tool, whereas the German Supreme Administrative Court was of the opposite view and expressly disagreed with the English Court of Appeal.[109]

One of the main advantages of references in the field of asylum and immigration is that preliminary rulings provide important insights into what is still a new area of EU competence. Making a reference also has the advantage of enabling the Court to receive observations from the Union Institutions and the Member States (including domestic courts), facilitating engagement at various levels of decision and policy making within the Union. Moreover, while there may be concerns of a "European" approach rather than an "International" approach to the interpretation of the Refugee Convention,[110] there is some evidence from the ECJ asylum case-law suggesting that its decisions may have a progressive effect from the perspective of asylum-seekers' human rights. For example, in *Bolbol* the ECJ followed the Opinion of AG Sharpston who adopted a more generous interpretation of Article 1D of the Geneva Convention concerning the status of refugees for Palestinians (which Article 12(1)(a) of the Qualification Directive refers to) than that provided by the UNHCR.

At a more practical level, concerns have been raised in relation to the delays (and costs) that can be caused by making a reference to pending cases before a

[104] See Ref. [96].

[105] See e.g. Case C-465/07, *Elgafaji and Elgafaji* [2009] ECR I-921; Cases C-175-179/08 *Abdulla and Others*, judgment of 2 March 2010, nyr; and C-31/09 *Bolbol* [2010] ECR I-5539.

[106] See e.g. the Czech Republic case, Supreme Administrative Court case of March 13, 2009, no 5 Azs 28: 2008, the UK case of *QD & AH (Iraq) (Appellants) v. Secretary of State for the Home Department (Respondent),* [2009] EWCA Civ 620; the German case of *Complainant v Respondent*, BVerwG 10 C 4.09 VGH 8 A 611/08.A, judgment of the Federal Administrative Court, 27 April 2010. All three decisions build on the *Elgafaji* ruling.

[107] See Ref. [97]; see also Ref. [98].

[108] See Council Directive 2004/83/EC as amended by Directive 2011/95/EU.

[109] See Judgment of the Federal Administrative Court (Bundesverwaltungsgericht) BVerwG 10 C 4.09 VGH 8 A 611/08.A, 27 April 2010, infra paras 22–34.

[110] It is noteworthy that the Statute of the ECJ does not permit third-party intervention despite the fact that the UNHCR for instance is considered as providing "valuable guidance" in the application and implementation of asylum law, see Recital 22 of the Recast Qualification Directive.

domestic court.[111] To that end an urgent procedure (PPU) was introduced in 2008 designed to reduce the delivery of a preliminary ruling in the AFSJ and thus applicable only in the areas covered by Title V of Part Three of the TFEU.[112] It is applied where the answer to the question raised is decisive as to the assessment of that person's legal situation or where the identity of the court having jurisdiction under EU law depends on the answer to the question referred for a preliminary ruling. To date, the ECJ has been dealing with a modest number of references in this area on the basis of the PPU.[113] Some concerns have been raised by several distinguished academics in relation to this fast-track procedure and, in particular, whether the Court is able to combine speed with an effective delivery of justice.[114] Among others, the lack of transparency of the overall decision-making process[115] exemplified by the brevity of the Court's rulings which do not seem to provide any discussion of the arguments of the parties and no reference to what was argued at the hearing, the lack of explanation as to why a PPU request has been rejected[116] and the non-publication of the AG's *prise de position* which is given orally but *in camera*.[117] The Rules of Procedure of the ECJ therefore have been amended.[118] The Preamble of the new Rules of Procedure explains the reasons for their

---

[111] By way of example, the *Bolbol* case took some 17 months from the reference in January 2009 to the judgment of the Court in June 2010. Similarly, in the *Abdulla* case the order of reference submitted by the German court made in early 2008 did not receive a ruling by the ECJ until 2 March 2010.

[112] The PPU procedure is governed by Article 23a of Protocol (No 3) on the Statute of the Court of Justice of the European Union (OJEU 2008 C 115, p. 210) and Articles 108–109 of the Rules of Procedure of the Court of Justice.

[113] In the field of asylum and border control, see e.g. Case C-357/09 PPU *Kadzoev*, Judgment of the Court (Grand Chamber) of 30 November 2009, nyr, and Case C-61/11 PPU *Hassen El Dridi alias Soufi Karim*, Judgment of the Court (First Chamber) of 28 April 2011, nyr, both concerning the Returns Directive (Directive 2008/115/EC), Case C-278/12 PPU *Atiqullah Adil v Minister voor Immigratie, Integratie en Asiel* Judgment of the Court (Second Chamber) of 19 July 2012, nyr, concerning the Schengen Borders Code. Judgment of the Court (Second Chamber) of 19 July 2012, nyr, concerning the Schengen Borders Code.

[114] See Ref. [99]; see also Ref. [100].

[115] This lack of transparency is in stark contrast with the Court's emphasis on openness as pivotal for ensuring greater legitimacy of the Union Institutions *vis-à-vis* EU citizens, see Joined Cases C-39/05 P and C-52/05 P, *Kingdom of Sweden and Maurizio Turco v Council of the European Union* [2008] ECR I-4723.

[116] Giving reasons for rejecting a PPU request would provide valuable guidance to other referring courts about when a PPU case is not "absolutely necessary;" Cfr. Joined Cases C-261/08 and C-348/08 *María Julia Zurita García, Aurelio Choque Cabrera v Delegado del Gobierno en la Región de Murcia* [2009] ECR I-10143 in which the PPU request was rejected (and thus the case was heard on the basis of the standard preliminary ruling procedure) with Case C-278/12 PPU *Atiqullah Adil v Minister voor Immigratie, Integratie en Asiel* Judgment of the Court (Second Chamber) of 19 July 2012, nyr, where the PPU request was accepted; both cases concerned the interpretation of Regulation 562/2006 (i.e. the Schengen Borders Code).

[117] See Ref. [101].

[118] The new provisions entered into force on 1st November 2012; see Article 210 of the Rules of Procedure of the Court of Justice of the European Union (OJ L 265/I, 29.9.2012).

amendment. First, the great number of preliminary proceedings in the Court's practice necessitated the adaptation of the rules, which were originally primarily tailored to direct actions, to its caseload.[119] The new rules take account of procedural economy considerations and, additionally, aim at simplifying complex procedures and ease certain procedural arrangements. Significantly, some changes have also been introduced in relation to the PPU procedure thus taking on board some of the afore-mentioned concerns about ensuring a fair hearing. Underlying these changes is also the broader consideration that the AFSJ has given rise to a considerable and increasing amount of legislative activity.[120] Moreover, Article 78 TFEU[121] links the development of a common policy on asylum (including the enactment of secondary legislation as well as EU agencies' migration management operations) with the compliance of the principle of *non-refoulement*, which goes beyond the obligation of the 1951 Convention. Article 78 TFEU, therefore, not only protects refugees from being sent back to places (mostly the country of origin) where their lives or freedoms could be threatened but also prohibits any act that prevents access to European territories and does not allow them to obtain the necessary protection.[122] This interpretation of Article 78 TFEU is confirmed by explicit reference to *non-refoulement* in various EU Directives such as the Asylum Procedures Directive (Directive 2005/85/EC), the Temporary Protection Directive (Directive 2001/55/EC)[123] and the Returns Directive (Directive 2008/115/EC).[124] Despite this, there have been problems of respecting the principle of *non-refoulement* either because of failure to transpose EU law into the domestic legal system[125] or because of inadequate access to procedures, poor reception conditions (also) at borders or points of entry amounting to ill-treatment, particularly of those asylum-seekers who are in a situation of vulnerability.[126] The European

[119] To this end, the new Rules introduced a separate, third Title on references for a preliminary ruling (Articles 93–118). In 2011, 423 references for a preliminary ruling were submitted to the ECJ of which 44 in the field of AFSJ (23 cases completed), see the 2011 Annual Report of the Court of Justice, Section D, Statistics of Judicial Activity of the Court of Justice, available at: http://curia.europa.eu/jcms/upload/docs/application/pdf/2012-06/ra2011_statistiques_cour_en.pdf.

[120] First, a case connected to another pending case assigned to a Judge Rapporteur can be assigned to the same Judge Rapporteur, even if he/she is not a member of the designated Chamber (Article 108 (2)). Second, another Member State can be invited to participate in the proceedings, in case the request for a preliminary ruling refers to an administrative procedure or to judicial proceedings in its territory (Article 109 (3)).

[121] Formerly Articles 63, points 1 and 2, and 64(2) EC.

[122] See Refs. [79–81], see footnote 83, at 695.

[123] For analysis and commentary, see Refs. [102–105]; see also Ref. [106, 107]

[124] For further analysis, see Refs. [108–112].

[125] See e.g. Case C-72/06 *Commission v Greece* [2007] ECR I-57.

[126] See e.g. Case of *Sharifi and others v Italy and Greece (Application No. 16643/09)* communicated on 13 July 2009; see also UN High Commissioner for Refugees, *Written Submission by the Office of the United Nations High Commissioner for Refugees in the Case of Sharifi and others v Italy and Greece (Application No. 16643/09)*, October 2009, Appl. No. 16643/09, available at: http://www.unhcr.org/refworld/docid/4afd25c32.html; ECRE, *Defending Refugees' Access to*

Commission has been endorsing a stronger human rights approach since the beginning of the second phase of CEAS with various Recast proposals calling for further harmonization and higher standards.[127] Furthermore, Article 18 of the EU Charter protecting the right to asylum equally seems to embrace a similar reading of Article 78 TFEU in consideration of the fact that the right to be granted asylum has become a subjective and enforceable right which not only must be respected but also protected in practice.[128]

Arguably, the ToL constitutes the culmination of a gradual but steady process of Europeanization or "de-nationalization"[129] of the decision-making process and a shift towards further transparency and democratization initiated by the ToA. Significantly, Article 67(1) TFEU provides that 'the Union shall constitute an area of freedom, security and justice with respect for fundamental rights and the different legal traditions and systems of the Member States' as well as the definition of a CEAS based on solidarity between Member States and which is fair towards TCNs. Article 15 TFEU reinforces the link between transparency and participatory democracy by stating that 'in order to promote good governance and ensure the participation of civil society, the Union's institutions, bodies and agencies shall conduct their work as openly as possible' and that the Parliament and the Council (when it considers and votes on a draft legislative act) shall meet in public. The role of national parliaments has also been strengthened following their monitoring of compliance of legislation in the AFSJ with the principle of subsidiarity[130] and the protocols on the role of the national parliaments in the EU and on the application of the principles of subsidiarity and proportionality.[131] In particular, they 'may participate in the evaluation mechanisms' for the implementation of Union policies in the AFSJ.[132]

(Footnote 126 continued)
Protection in Europe, December 2007, available at: http://www.ecre.org/topics/areas-of-work/access-to-europe/95-defending-refugees-access-to-protection-in-europe.html.

[127] See Refs. [113, 114].

[128] This can be inferred from the reasoning of the Court in *Bolbol*, C-31/09 *Bolbol* [2010] ECR I-5539, examined above and also, more recently, from the ruling in Case C-245/11 *K v Bundesasylamt (Austria)*, Judgment of the Court (Grand Chamber), nyr, and Case C-528/11 *Zuheyr Freyeh Halaf v Darzhavna agentsia za bezhantsite pri Ministerski*, nyr, Judgment of 30 May 2013.

[129] By "de-nationalization" I refer to the demise of individual states' centrality in decision-making most well-represented by conventional approaches to national sovereignty. I am not suggesting a clear-cut supranationalization over and beyond intergovermentalist forms of decision-making at EU level, the premise being that states in a post-Westphalian era can only survive as a collectivity.

[130] See Articles 5(3) TEU and 69 TFEU.

[131] See Protocols 1 and 2.

[132] See Article 12(c) TEU.

As regards the substantive scope of the CEAS, Article 78(2) TFEU uses the latter term to include the following:

- a uniform status of asylum
- a uniform status of subsidiary protection
- a common system of temporary protection
- common procedures for the granting and withdrawing of uniform asylum or subsidiary protection status
- criteria and mechanisms for determining the responsible state
- standards concerning the conditions for the reception of applicants for asylum or subsidiary protection
- partnership and cooperation with third countries for the purpose of managing inflows of people applying for asylum or subsidiary or temporary protection.

According to the European Commission the development of CEAS entails progressive legislation, leading to a shift from "voluntary" to "mandatory," and an abolition of opt-out clauses and finally to a "full" harmonization of procedures, criteria and mechanisms as well as standards mentioned in Article 78 TFEU. Under Article 78 TFEU the term CEAS will rank as a primary EU law concept allowing for a systematic approach to the asylum *acquis*.[133]

2.1.4 *The Significance of the EU Charter of Fundamental Rights and Freedoms in Strengthening Protection Seekers' Rights*

With the entry into force of the ToL, the EU Charter has acquired the same legal status of the EU Treaties with the effect that it has become legally binding for all the EU institutions, bodies and agencies and for the EU Member States' actions within the scope of EU law.[134] The EU Charter sets out in a single text a range of civil, political, economic and social rights of European citizens and all persons resident in the EU. It has thus increased the visibility of existing rights.[135] As noted by Iglesias Sánchez 'the Charter has improved the centrality and weight of fundamental rights, reinforcing both their visibility in the legal discourse of the Court and their role as parameters of *constitutionality*.'[136]

Until the adoption of the EU Charter we were accustomed to understanding the protection of fundamental human rights as belonging to two separate universes: on the one hand, that of national constitutional settlements and, on the other hand, that

---

[133] See Hailbronner, see footnote 63, p. 8.

[134] See Article 6 (1) TEU; for critical analysis, see Ref. [115].

[135] See Ref. [116], at 1204.

[136] See Ref. [117], at 1576.

of international, including regional, human rights instruments.[137] With the entry into force of the ToL, the entitlement to rights no longer depends on either national constitutional settlements or on international human rights treaties (with all the difficulties attendant on accessing those rights).[138] Already prior to the ToL, at a time when the EU Charter was still a persuasive legal instrument for statutory interpretation, Advocate General (AG) Maduro in his Opinion in the *Elgafaji* case,[139] stated that the EU Charter had a dual function: 'In the first place, it may create the presumption of the existence of a right which will then require confirmation of its existence either in the constitutional traditions common to the Member States or in the provisions of the ECHR. In the second place, where a right is identified as a fundamental right protected by the Community legal order, the EU Charter provides a particularly useful instrument for determining the content, scope and meaning to be given to that right.'

The EU Charter is not limited in its scope of application to Union citizens but also extends to TCNs. The significant novelty of the EU Charter's provisions is that only a few are limited to EU citizens, which are mainly to be found in Title V. However, even in this chapter, there are very important rights to which any person is entitled to. For example, Article 41 of the EU Charter contains a right to good administration and it provides that: 'every person has the right to have his or her affairs handed impartially, fairly and within a reasonable time by the institutions and bodies of the Union.' When referring to the institutions and bodies of the Union it also includes national authorities when they are carrying out EU law (as per Article 51 of the EU Charter). Consequently, asylum-seekers can equally rely on Article 41 of the EU Charter for requesting that his or her claim be dealt with in an impartial and fair manner and within a reasonable period of time. This argument is further buttressed by the fact that asylum law and policy is now clearly within the remit of EU law.[140] By the same token, asylum-seekers can also rely on Article 47 of the EU Charter, which provides for the right to an effective remedy and to a fair trial.[141]

Moreover, Article 18 of the EU Charter states that: 'The right to asylum shall be guaranteed with due respect for the rules of the Geneva Convention of 28 July 1951 and the Protocol of 31 January 1967 relating to the status of refugees and in accordance with the Treaty on European Union and the Treaty on the Functioning of the European Union (hereinafter referred to as "the Treaties").' Gil-Bazo traces the roots of Article 18 of the EU Charter back to Article 14 of the 1948 Universal Declaration of Human Rights (UDHR).[142] By examining the Charter's *travaux*

---

[137] See Ref. [118].

[138] Idem.

[139] See Opinion of AG Maduro in Case C-465/07 *Elgafaji and Elgafaji* [2009] ECR I-921.

[140] E.g., see the Qualification Directive 2004/83 and the Procedures Directive 2005/85.

[141] E.g., C-175/08 *Abdulla* case where the ECJ refers, among other things, to the respect of the rights protected in the EU Charter.

[142] See Ref. [119].

préparatoires and *explanations* drafted by the Presidium[143] as well as the constitutional traditions of Member States, she argues that the EU Charter seems to have gone beyond Article 14 UDHR[144] and the right to be granted asylum has become a subjective and enforceable right the protection of which all individuals with an international protection need are entitled under the Union's legal order, provided that their protection grounds are established by international law, irrespective of whether they are found in the Refugee Convention or in any other international human rights instrument.[145] The combination of Article 18 of the EU Charter and Article 78 TFEU goes beyond a mere recognition of the existence of the right to asylum and of its respect. It now weighs on the EU and its Member States as a true "positive obligation" implied by the need to "guarantee" the right to asylum. In accordance with the law of the ECHR as developed by the Strasbourg Court, the concept of "positive obligation" here means an obligation to "ensure" which goes beyond an obligation "not to do," that of the classic prohibition of breaching the Geneva Convention.[146] Hence, the obligations derived from Article 18 of the EU Charter are not only satisfied by the principle of non-*refoulement.* The former requires additionally that an effective benefit of that protection, including an appropriate status, must be ensured. Moreover, the combined provisions of Article 18 of the EU Charter and Article 78 TFEU effectively "constitutionnalize"[147] the material scope of the right to asylum in the EU. In this context, AG Maduro stated in *Elgafaji* that the Qualification Directive aims to assert the fundamental right to asylum.[148] Furthermore, Peers argues that the right to asylum should be considered to be a general principle of EU law due to its recognition in many national constitutions.[149] *A fortiori* a return to a country which does not grant status is incompatible with Article 18 of the EU Charter given that it provides that the right to asylum must be guaranteed (not merely the "right to seek" asylum as per Article 14 UDHR).[150]

However, there is also another reading of the provision contained in Article 18 of the EU Charter. According to this interpretation, the right to asylum does not have autonomous legal content: pursuant to the provision in Article 18 of the EU Charter the right to asylum has to be guaranteed within the legal framework of the Geneva Convention and EU law (including the rules of interpretation provided by Article 6(1) TEU, Title VII of the EU Charter and the case law of the ECJ).

---

143 See Ref. [120].

144 On Article 14 UDHR, Gammeltoft-Hansen and Gammeltoft-Hansen say that the provision does seem to require a right to an asylum procedure of some kind for it to be meaningful, see Ref. [121].

145 See Ref. [119], see footnote 142, at 48 and 50.

146 See Ref. [122], at p. 430.

147 Ibidem, at p. 431.

148 See AG Maduro Opinion in C-465/07 *Elgafaji v. Staatssecretaris van Justitie* [2009] ECR I-921, para. 30.

149 See Ref. [123].

150 See Ref. [124], at 36.

Consequently, following this reading Article 18 of the EU Charter cannot be interpreted as meaning that it produces direct effects and that it creates individual rights which national courts must protect, as the provision does not ensure a clear and unconditional right. What it means rather is its implementation is made conditional to the adoption of EU secondary legislation and/or measures enacted under national law. The fact that Article 18 of the EU Charter is subject to different interpretations may explain why the ECJ to date has been reluctant to pronounce itself on the exact content of the right to asylum.

Article 19 of the EU Charter is the other relevant provision for asylum-seekers. According to the EU Charter's Explanations,[151] paragraph 1 of this Article has the same meaning and scope as Article 4 of the Protocol No 4 to the ECHR concerning collective expulsion. Its purpose is to guarantee that every decision is based on a specific examination and that no single measure can be taken to expel all persons having the nationality of a particular State.[152] Paragraph 2 incorporates case-law from the ECtHR regarding Article 3 of the ECHR, chiefly, that the prohibition of collective expulsion in international law is based on two basic principles, namely the prohibition of discrimination and the prohibition of arbitrariness. It also extends the fundamental principle of *non-refoulement* to all cases of removal, extradition and deportation where a person would be sent to a country where there is a real risk of being executed, tortured or subjected to other inhuman or degrading treatment or punishment.

2.1.5 From "Minimum" to "More Favourable Standards" to "Common": Where Do We Draw the Line?

Despite the official shift in focus from "minimum" to "common" standards that the creation and further development of CEAS has generated and that is clearly visible in the recast proposals of the existing asylum Directives,[153] the push for further harmonization has not entailed an abandonment *tout cours* of flexibility and a margin of appreciation on the part of the Member States.[154] As noted by

[151] See Praesidium of the European Convention [120], see footnote 143.

[152] See also Article 13 of the ICCPR.

[153] For instance, in the revised Reception Conditions Directive there is reference to "standards" rather than "minimum standards" reflecting the wording of the ToL. However, Member States will still be free to set "more favourable provisions" for asylum-seekers (e.g. Article 4); similarly with regard to the revised Asylum Procedures Directive where the focus shifted to setting "common procedures" rather than "minimum standards", again reflecting the revised wording of the ToL. However, Member States will still be free to set "more favourable provisions" for asylum procedures (e.g. Article 5).

[154] In examining the Asylum Procedures Directive, Vedsted-Hansen argues that Member States are willing to accept a relatively high degree of harmonization in some policy areas, while in others persist in defending domestic legislation, thereby in effect undermining the minimum

Hailbronner, it seems unlikely that by adopting the ToL Member States were prepared to completely give up their specific concepts of accommodating protection needs.[155]

The changes introduced by the ToL focusing on the adoption of "common policies"[156] seem to indicate that further legislation in asylum is not limited to "minimum standards." In particular, the reference to "standards" would seem to indicate a departure from the lowest common level of all EU Member States. In spite of their different meaning, the term "minimum standards" has often been used in close connection with the "more favourable standards" clause which is explicitly included in all Directives.[157] Basically, irrespective of the more favourable treatment clauses of the Directives it is assumed that the provisions of the Directives admit a deviation in favour of TCNs whose rights and duties are regulated by the Directives. As the term itself suggests, "minimum standards" refers to legislation providing for a set of "minimum rules" which must be observed by the Member States and which does not have a harmonizing objective. The term "more favourable standards" instead permits Member States to go beyond the general standards established in CEAS. While *prima facie* it may appear as a better clause, this term has been problematic in practice.[158] In the first place, Member States have used this clause to argue that by maintaining more favourable national laws no transposition of asylum Directives was needed with the unwanted result of having either a partial or full non-transposition of asylum Directive provisions.[159] Linked to this, allowing Member States to maintain substantially different "higher" standards concerning the processing of asylum-seekers and the criteria on eligibility potentially undermines CEAS (and negates its harmonization objective) and the concept of a uniform status and, furthermore, it does not deter secondary movements making the idea of a general system of mutual recognition of asylum decisions very difficult to achieve. Hence, as pointed out by Symes the EU's aspiration of harmonization 'does not yet reflect the reality on the ground. The question that confronts the refugee lawyer is whether there is any tenable legal challenge based on failures to adequately implement the Directives.'[160]

(Footnote 154 continued)
harmonization stipulated by Article 63 EC, for a combination of *regulatory tradition* and *calculated evasion* [emphasis added], see Ref. [60], see footnote 66, at p. 262.

155 See Ref. [125].

156 See chapter 2, Title V, Part Three.

157 For examples, see footnote 153.

158 See Ref. [125], see footnote 155, at p. 4.

159 Examples are the transposition of provisions relating to the refugee definition and/or the definition of persons eligible for subsidiary protection or the transposition of mandatory provisions on refusal or termination of refugee and subsidiary protection status in the event that there are no provisions under national law. See also Ref. [126], 4.

160 See M. Symes, see footnote 150, at 29.

From a narrower perspective, it may be questioned the extent to which it is possible to apply the concept of "more favourable standards" to provisions which contain obligatory restrictions concerning the acquisition and exercise of rights under the Directives. Most Directives' provisions are drafted in mandatory language and use the word "shall." Moreover, even in cases where the provisions allow for Member States' discretion and include the word "may" there is still a degree of obligation implicit in them in so far as Member States must not exclude certain approaches to interpretation. A 2002 legal opinion of the Council's legal service on the mandatory nature of the draft Qualification Directive's provisions confirms this approach.[161] In particular, the legal opinion provided that, under certain circumstances and from the content of a given provision, the use of the word "may" can also include an obligation from which no derogation is possible. Article 5(1) of the Qualification Directive is an example of the latter, where it provides that a well-founded fear of being persecuted "may be based" on events that have taken place since the applicant left the country of origin.[162] The above legal opinion also stated that the term "shall" may provide minimum standards in relation to the rights and benefits of TCNs which leave it open for Member States to grant more favourable treatment to those persons. At the same time, it seems that minimum standards will not permit derogations if according to the purpose and content of the provision the derogation would be incompatible with the aim of harmonization. In these circumstances, allowing derogations could impede the effective implementation of the Directive owing to the potentially negative effects on other Member States. On a more general note, it could also be argued that a further difficulty with these concepts is that, due to the complexity in establishing their clear boundary, the current powers of the Commission to initiate infringement proceedings before the ECJ against a Member State, which fails to comply with EU asylum law, is weakened.

Two UNHCR comparative studies on the implementation of the Qualification Directive in selected Member States[163] and the Asylum Procedures Directive[164] show divergent outcomes of comparable asylum applications in different Member States due to the significant variations in recognition practices. With regard to asylum procedures, the UNHCR study found that the Directive has not achieved the harmonization of legal standards or practices across the EU it was purported to achieve. The main reason is the degree of flexibility and wide margin of discretion allowed by the Directive's provisions combined different interpretations of the rules and different approaches to their application by the Member States.

The problems and flaws inherent in the EU asylum Directives adopted during the CEAS' first phase have been clearly acknowledged by the European Commission. In both the 2007 Green Paper on the *future Common European Asylum*

---

[161] See Ref. [127].

[162] See Ref. [128], at 17.

[163] See Ref. [129].

[164] See Ref. [129], see footnote 159.

System[165] and the 2008 Policy Plan on *Asylum*,[166] the Commission suggested ways to minimize the margin for divergent interpretation and application in the Member States through a higher degree of harmonization of protection standards thus ensuring access to protection under equivalent conditions across the EU, an approach which is reflected in its recast proposals.

References

1. Gallie WB (1956) Essentially contested concepts. Proc Aristotelian Soc 56:167–198
2. Besson S (2004) Sovereignty in conflict. Eur Integr Online Papers (EIoP) 8(15):1–50
3. Walker N (2004) In search of the area of freedom, security and justice: a constitutional Odissey. In: Walker N (ed) Europe's area of freedom, security and justice. OUP, Oxford, pp 3–37
4. Bartelson J (1995) A genealogy of sovereignty. Cambridge University Press, Cambridge, p 6
5. Goodwin-Gill GS, McAdam J (2009) The refugee in international law. OUP, Oxford, p 6
6. Diez T (1997) International Ethics and European Integration: Federal State or Network Horizon? Altern Glob Local, Polit 22:287–312
7. Kostakopoulou D (2002) Floating sovereignty: a pathology or a necessary means of state evolution? Oxford J Legal Stud 22(1):135–156
8. MacCormick N (1993) Beyond the sovereign state. Mod Law Rev 56(1):1–18
9. MacCormick N (1999) Questioning sovereignty: law, state, and nation in the European commonwealth. OUP, Oxford
10. Guild E (2012) Examining the European geography of refugee protection: exclusions, limitations and exceptions from the 1967 protocol to the present. Eur Hum Rights Law Rev 17(4):413
11. Sarooshi D (2003–2004) The essentially contested nature of the concept of sovereignty: implications for the exercise by international organizations of delegated powers of government. Mich J Int Law 24(4):1107–1140
12. French D (2009) Finding autonomy in international environmental law and governance. J Environ Law 21(2):255–289
13. Krasner SD (2003–2004) The hole in the whole: sovereignty, shared sovereignty and international law. Mich J Int Law 25(4):1075–1102
14. Arrighi G, Silver BJ et al (1999) Chaos and governance in the modern world system. University of Minnesota Press, Minneapolis
15. Beck U (1992) Risk society: towards a new modernity. Sage, New Delhi
16. Raz J (1980) The concept of a legal system: an introduction to the theory of legal system. Clarendon Press, Oxford, pp 139–140
17. Krasner SD (1999) Sovereignty: organised hypocrisy. Princeton University Press, Princeton
18. Brunsson N (2003) Organised hypocrisy. In: Cziamiawska B, Sevón G (eds) The northern lights: organization theory in Scandinavia. Liber, Stockholm, pp 201–222
19. Huysmans J (2004) A Foucaultian view on spill-over: freedom and security in the EU. J Int Rel Dev 7:294–318
20. Huysmans J (2000) The European Union and the securitisation of migration. J Comm Market Stud 38(5):751–777

---

[165] See Ref. [130].

[166] See Ref. [131].

21. Balzacq T (2008) The policy tools of securitization: information exchange, EU foreign and interior policies. J Comm Market Stud 46(1):75–100
22. European Council (2010) The Stockholm programme—an open and secure Europe serving and protecting citizens (2010/C 115/01), OJ 4.5.2010 N. C 115/1 §6
23. Vanheule D (2012) The Multi-faceted role of law in the development of European asylum and migration policy. In: Gortázar C et al (eds) European migration and asylum policies: coherence or contradiction? Bruylant, Brussels, pp. 92–94
24. Goodwin-Gill GS (2012) Europe: a place to seek, to be granted, and to enjoy asylum?' In: Gortázar C et al (eds) European migration and asylum policies: coherence or contradiction? Bruylant, Brussels, pp. 33–43
25. Stürmer M (2013) Amici Riluttanti in Nome dell'Europa. In: La Repubblica, 6 May 2013
26. Carrera S (2011) The impact of the treaty of Lisbon over EU policies on migration, asylum and borders: the struggles over the ownership of the Stockholm programme. In Guild E, Minderhoud P, Cholewinski R (eds) The First decade of eu migration and asylum law. Martinus Nijhoff Publishers, Leiden, pp 229–254
27. European Commission (2010) Communication on delivering an area of freedom, security and justice for Europe's citizens: action plan implementing the Stockholm programme, COM (2010) 171 final
28. Council of the European Union (2010) Draft council conclusions on the commission communication 'delivering an area of freedom, security and justice for Europe's citizens—action plan implementing the Stockholm programme' (COM(2010) 171 final), 9935/10, Brussels, 19 May 2010
29. Guild E (2012) From persecution to management of populations: governmentality and the common European asylum system. Nijmegen Migration Law Working Paper Series 2012/04
30. Hailbronner K (2010) Introduction into the EU immigration and asylum law. In: Hailbronner K (ed) EU Immigration and asylum law—commentary. Hart, Oxford, pp 1–27
31. Peers S (2005) Human rights, asylum and European community law. Refugee Surv Q 24(2):24–38, at 29–30
32. UNHCR (1979) Handbook on procedures and criteria for determining refugee Status under the 1951 convention and 1967 protocol relating to the status of refugees, HCR/IP/4/Eng/REV.1, Reedited, Geneva, January 1992. Available via http://www.unhcr.org/3d58e13b4.html
33. UNHCR (2003) manual on refugee protection and the European convention of human rights, (April 2003, Updated August 2006). August 2006. Available via http://www.refworld.org/docid/3f4cd5c74.html
34. International Law Association (2002) International law association, resolution 6/2002 on refugee procedures (Declaration on International Minimum Standards for Refugee Procedures), 6 April 2002,6/2002. Available via: http://www.refworld.org/docid/4280b2404.html
35. Kostakopoulou D (2002) "Integrating" Non-EU migrants in the European Union: ambivalent legacies and mutating paradigms. Columbia J Eur Law 8:181–201
36. Staffans I (2012) Evidence in European asylum procedures. Martinus Nijhoff Publishers, Leiden
37. Battjes H (2006) European asylum law and international law. Martinus Nijhoff Publishers, Leiden
38. Boccardi I (2002) Europe and refugees: towards an EU asylum policy. Kluwer Law International, The Hague
39. Boeles P et al (2009) European migration law. Intersentia, Antwerp
40. Guild E (2006) The Europeanization of Europe's asylum policy. Int J Refugee Law 3–4:630–651
41. Hailbronner K (2004) Asylum law in the context of a European migration policy. In: Walker N (ed) Europe's area of freedom, security and justice. OUP, Oxford, pp. 41–142
42. Ippolito F, Velluti S (2011) The recast process of the eu asylum system: a balancing act between efficiency and fairness. Refugee Surv Q 30(3):24–62, at 24–32

43. Peers S (2006) From black market to constitution: the development of the institutional framework for ec immigration and asylum law. In Peers S, Rogers N (eds) EU Immigration and Asylum Law. Martinus Nijhoff Publishers, Leiden, pp. 19–46
44. Peers S (2006) The EU institutions and title IV. In Peers S, Rogers N (eds) EU immigration and asylum law. Martinus Nijhoff Publishers, Leiden, pp 47–80
45. Peers S (2011) EU justice and home affairs law. OUP, Oxford
46. Staffans I (2008) Convergence and mutual recognition in European Asylum law. In: Klabbers J, Sellers M (eds) The internationalization of law and legal education. Springer, Dordrecht, p. 150
47. Austin J(1995) [1832] The province of jurisprudence determined. W. Rumble ed, Cambridge
48. Bodin J (1962) The six books of a Commonweale. Harvard University Press, Kenneth Douglas McRae ed
49. Hobbes T (1947) Leviathan. Macmillan, Michael Oakeshott ed
50. Schmitt C (1922) Politische Theologie. Vier Kapitel zur Lehre von der Souveränität. Duncker and Humblot, Munich and Leipzig
51. de Vattel E (1792) The law of nations, or, the principles of the law of nature, applied to the conduct and affairs of nations and sovereigns. Luke White, Dublin
52. Harlow C, Guild E (2001) Implementing amsterdam. Hart, Oxford
53. Byme R, Gregor N, Vedsted-Hansen J (2002) New asylum countries? Migration control and refugee protection in an enlarged European Union. Kluwer International, The Hague
54. Fletcher M (2003) EU governance techniques in the creation of a common European policy on immigration and asylum. European Public Law 9(4):533–562
55. European Commission (2007) Green paper on the future common European asylum system. COM(2007) 301 final
56. Fuller LL (1969) The morality of law. Yale University Press, New Haven pp. 33–94
57. French D (2009) Global justice and the (Ir)relevance of indeterminacy. Chin J Int Law 8(3):593–619
58. Leib EJ (2006) Responsibility and social/political choices about choice: or, one way to be a true non-voluntarist. Law Philos 25(4):453–488
59. Thielemann ER (2003) Between interests and norms: explaining burden-sharing in the European Union. J Refugee Stud 16(3):253–273
60. Vedsted-Hansen J (2011) Common EU standards on asylum—optional harmonization and exclusive procedures? In: Guild E, Minderhoud P, Cholewinski R (eds) The first decade of EU migration and Asylum law. Martinus Nijhoff Publishers, Leiden, pp. 255–271
61. Brouwer E (2011) Effective remedies for third country nationals in EU law: justice accessible to all? In: Guild E, Minderhoud P, Cholewinski R (eds) The first decade of EU migration and asylum law. Martinus Nijhoff Publishers, Leiden, pp 375–400
62. The Hague Programme (2004) Strengthening freedom, security and justice in the European Union, Annex I to the presidency conclusions of the European council 4–5 November 2004
63. Stockholm Programme (2010) An open and secure Europe serving and protecting the citizens, adopted by the Council of the European Union 10–11 December 2009 (final draft 2 December 2009, Council doc. 17024/09), published in OJ C 115/1, 4 May 2010
64. Council of the European Union (2008) European pact on immigration and asylum (13440/08), 24 September 2008
65. European Commission (2010) Communication from the commission to the european parliament, the council, the european economic and social committee and the committee of the regions of 20 April 2010—Delivering an area of freedom, security and justice for Europe's citizens—action plan implementing the Stockholm programme COM (2010) 171 final
66. Van Selm J (2005) European refugee policy: is there such a thing? UNHCR research Paper No. 115, www.unhcr.org/research/RESEARCH/42943ce02.pdf
67. Guild E (2003) International Terrorism and eu immigration, asylum and borders policy: the unexpected victims of 11 September 2001. Eur Foreign Affairs Rev 8(3):331–346

68. Nicholson F (2006) Challenges of forging a common european asylum in line with international obligations. In: Peers an S, Rogers N (eds) EU Immigration and Asylum Law. Kluwer Law International, The Hague, pp 505–538 at p. 507
69. Costello C (2005) The asylum procedures directive and the proliferation of safe third countries: deterrence, deflection and the dismantling of international protection? Eur J Migr Law 7(1):35–70
70. Hathaway JC (1993) Harmonizing for whom? The devaluation of refugee protection in an Era of European economic integration. Cornell Int Law J 26(3):719–735, at 723
71. Zetter R (2007) More labels, fewer refugees: remaking the refugee label in an Era of globalization. J Refugee Stud 20(2):172–192, at 180
72. Uçarer EM (2006) Burden-shirking, burden-shifting, and burden-sharing in the emergent european asylum regime. Int Polit 43(2):219–240
73. European Commission (2008) Proposal for a regulation of the european parliament and of the council establishing the criteria and mechanisms for determining the member state responsible for examining an application for international protection lodged in one of the Member States by a third-country national or a stateless person COM (2008) 820
74. European Commission (2008a) Proposal for a regulation of the European parliament and of the council concerning the establishment of 'Eurodac' for the comparison of fingerprints for the effective application of the regulation (EC) No 343/2003 COM (2008) 825
75. European Commission (2008b) Proposal for a directive of the European parliament and of the council laying down minimum standards for the reception of asylum-seekers, COM(2008) 815
76. European Commission (2009) Proposal for a directive of the European parliament and of the council on minimum standards for the qualification and status of third country nationals or stateless persons as beneficiaries of international protection and the content of the protection granted COM (2009) 551 final
77. European Commission (2009a) Proposal for a directive of the European Parliament and of the council on minimum standards on procedures in member States for granting and withdrawing international protection COM (2009) 554/4 final
78. Hailbronner K (ed) (2010) EU immigration and asylum law—commentary. Hart, Oxford
79. Adinolfi A (2009) Riconoscimento dello status di rifugiato e della protezione sussidiaria: verso un sistema comune europeo? Rivista di Diritto Internazionale 92(3):669–696
80. Allain J (2001) The Jus Cogens Nature of Non-Refoulement. Int J Refugee Law 13(4): 533–558
81. Chan PCW (2006) The protection of refugees and internally displaced persons: non-refoulement under customary international law? Int J Human Rights 10(3):231–239
82. European Parliament and Council of the European Union (2010) Regulation 439/2010 of the European Parliament and of the Council of 19 May 2010 establishing a European Asylum Support Office, OJ L 132/11, 29 May2010
83. Guild et al E (2011) Implementation of the EU charter of fundamental rights and its impact on EU home affairs agencies. Frontex, Europol and the European asylum support office, Study for the European parliament, DG for Internal Policies, Civil Liberties, Justice and Home Affairs, Policy Department C: Citizens' Rights and Constitutional Affairs, PE 453.196
84. Levy C (2010) Refugees, Europe, Camps/State of Exception: "Into the Zone", The European Union and extraterritorial processing of migrants, refugees, and asylum-seekers (Theories and Practice). Refugee Survey Q 29(1):92–119
85. Amnesty International (2011) The European asylum support office (EASO): closing the protection gap in europe?', Amnesty international, London, March 2011. Available via http://www.amnesty.eu/content/assets/Doc2011/EASO_March_2010_Medium_Res.pdf
86. Guiraudon V (2004) Immigration and Asylum: A High Politics Agenda. In: Dinan D, Green Cowles M (eds) Developments in the European Union 2. Palgrave MacMillan, London, pp. 160–180

87. Geddes A (2002) The EU migration regime's effects on European welfare states. In: Lavenex S, Uçarer EM (eds) Migration and the externalities of European integration. Lexington Books, Lanham, pp 195–207
88. European Parliament and Council of the European Union (2009), Regulation (EC) No 810/2009 of the European Parliament and of the Council of 13 July 2009 establishing a Community Code on Visas (Visa Code), OJ L243/1, 15.9.2009
89. European Parliament and Council of the European Union (2010) Regulation (EU) No 265/2010 of the European parliament and of the council of 25 March 2010 amending the convention Implementing the Schengen agreement and regulation (EC) No 562/2006 as regards movement of persons with a long-stay visa, OJ L85/1, 31.3.2010 (Schengen Borders Code)
90. Peers S et al (eds) (2012) EU immigration and asylum law—volume 1 on visas and border controls. Martin Nijhoff, Leiden
91. Kostakopoulou D (2010) An open and secure Europe? Fixity and fissures in the area of freedom, security and justice after Lisbon and Stockholm. Eur Secur 19(2):151–167
92. Peers S (2008) Legislative update: EU immigration and asylum competence and decision-making in the treaty of Lisbon. Eur J Migr Law 10:219–247, at 235
93. Peers S(2012) The revised directive on asylum-seekers' Reception Conditions: The Member States Hit Rock-Bottom' Statewatch Analysis, March 2012. Available via http://www.statewatch.org/analyses/no-172-reception.pdf
94. Peers S (2011) Revised EU asylum proposals: lipstick on a pig. Statewatch Analysis June 2011. Available via: http://www.statewatch.org/analyses/no-132-asylum.pdf
95. Peers S (2012) The revised asylum procedures directive: keeping standards low Statewatch Analysis, May 2012. Available via http://www.statewatch.org/analyses/no-178-asylum-procedures.pdf
96. Peers S (2011) Mission Accomplished? EU Justice and Home Affairs Law After the Treaty of Lisbon. Comm Market Law Rev 48:681–685
97. European Commission (2004) Report from the commission to the European parliament and to the council on the application of directive 2004/83/EC of 29 April 2004, COM (2010) 314 final
98. UNHCR (2010) Improving asylum procedures: comparative analysis and recommendations for law and practice, March 2010. Available via http://www.unhcr.org/4ba9d99d9.html
99. Barnard C (2009) The PPU: is it worth the candle? An early assessment. Eur Law Rev 34(2):281–297
100. Rosas A (2008/09) Justice in haste, justice denied? The European court of justice and the area of freedom, security and justice. Cambridge Yearb Eur Legal Stud 11:1–13
101. Committee on Legal Affairs (2007) Rapporteur diana Wallis, report on the draft council decision amending the protocol on the statute of the court of justice with regard to the treatment of questions referred for a preliminary ruling concerning the area of freedom, security and justice, (11824/2007-C6-0292/2007-2007/0812(CNS), of 21.11.2007. Available via http://www.europarl.europa.eu/sides/getDoc.do?pubRef=-//EP//NONSGML+REPORT+A6-2007-0451+0+DOC+PDF+V0//EN
102. Kerber K (2002) The temporary protection directive. Eur J Migr Law 4(2):193–214
103. Noll G, Gunneflo M (2007) Directive 2001/55—temporary protection—synthesis report. Odysseus Study on the 'Conformity Checking of the Transposition by Member States of 10 EC Directives in the Sector of Asylum and Immigration,' Brussels 2007
104. Van Selm J (2001) Temporarily protecting displaced persons or offering the possibility to start a new life in the European Union. Eur J Migr Law 3(1):23–35
105. Skordas A (2010) Council Directive 2001/55/EC of 20 July 2001 on minimum standards for giving temporary protection in the event of a mass influx of displaced persons and on measures promoting a balance of efforts between Member States in receiving such persons and bearing the consequences thereof. In: Hailbronner K (ed) EU Immigration and Asylum Law—Commentary. Hart, Oxford, pp 803–870

106. Türk V, Edwards A, Braeunlich M (2013) Introductory note to the San Remo summary conclusions on temporary protection. Int J Refugee Law 25(1):175–177
107. UNHCR Division of International Protection (2013) UNHCR roundtable on temporary protection international institute of humanitarian law—summary conclusions on temporary protection. Int J Refugee Law 25(1):178–186
108. Acosta Arcarazo D (2011) The good, the bad and the ugly in eu migration law: is the European parliament becoming bad and ugly? (The Adoption of Directive 2008/115: the Returns Directive). In: Guild E, Minderhoud P, Cholewinski R (eds) The first decade of eu migration and asylum law. Martinus Nijhoff Publishers, Leiden, pp. 179–206
109. Baldaccini A (2009) The return and removal of irregular migrants under eu law: an analysis of the return directive. Eur J Migr Law 11(1):1–17
110. ECRE (2009) Information note on the directive 2008/115/EC of the European parliament and of the council of 16 December 2008 on common standards and procedures in Member States for returning illegally staying third-country nationals, 7 January 2009, CO7/1/2009/Ext/MDM. Available at http://www.refworld.org/docid/496c61e42.html
111. Schieffer M (2010) Directive 2008/115/EC of the European parliament and of the council of 16 December 2008 on common standards and procedures in member states for returning illegally staying third-country nationals. In: Hailbronner K (ed) EU Immigration and asylum law—Commentary. Hart, Oxford, pp 1489–1552
112. UNHCR (2008) Position on the proposal for a directive on common standards and procedures in member states for returning illegally staying third-country nationals. June 2008. Available via http://www.unhcr.org/4d948a1f9.pdf
113. European Commission (2008) Communication from the commission to the European parliament, the council, the European economic and social committee and the committee of the regions, policy plan on asylum. an integrated approach to protection across the EU, (COM (2008) 360 final)
114. White R (2011) A new era for human Rights in the European Union? Yearb Eur Law 30(1):100–130
115. Schütze R (2011) Three "Bills of Rights" for the European Union. Yearb Eur Law 30(1):131–158
116. Lord Goldsmith QC (2001) A charter of rights, freedoms and principles. Comm Market Law Rev 38(5):1201–1216
117. Iglesias Sánchez S (2012) The court and the charter: the impact of the entry into force of the Lisbon treaty on the ecj's approach to fundamental rights. Comm Market Law Rev 49(5):1565–1612
118. Guild E (2010) Fundamental rights and EU citizenship. Global jean Monnet/European community studies association world conference on The European Union after the Treaty of Lisbon. pp 25–26 May 2010 July 2010
119. Gil Bazo M-T (2008) The charter of fundamental rights of the European Union and the right to be granted asylum in the Union's Law. Refugee Survey Q 27(3):33–52
120. Praesidium of the European Convention (2007) Explanations relating to the charter of fundamental rights, OJ C303, 14.12.2007, P. 17 (Amended version)
121. Gammeltoft-Hansen T, Gammeltoft-Hansen H (2008) The right to seek- revisited. on the un human rights declaration article 14 and access to asylum procedures in the EU. Eur J Migr Law 10(4):439–459
122. Labayle H (2010) The impact of article 18 of the charter of fundamental rights', section 1, part 3, european parliament, directorate-general for internal policies, policy department c, citizens' rights and constitutional affairs, 'setting up a common european asylum system. Report on the application of existing instruments and proposals for the new system PE 425.622. Brussels 2010:427–433
123. Peers S (2011) EU justice and home affairs law. OUP, 3rd ed, Oxford, p. 98
124. Symes M (2010) Challenging "Dublin" removals - human rights and European law arguments. J Immigr Asylum Nationality Law 24(1):29–38

125. Hailbronner K (2008) Towards a common european asylum system—assessment and proposals-elements to be implemented for the establishment of an efficient and coherent system. Briefing Note for the Directorate-General Internal Policies, Policy Department C, Citizens Rights and Constitutional Affairs, European Parliament, September 2008, PE 408.201, p. 2
126. UNHCR (2010) Improving asylum procedures: comparative analysis and recommendations for law and practice. A UNHCR research project on the application of key provisions of the Asylum Procedures Directive in Selected Member States, Brussels: UNHCR 2010. Available via http://www.unhcr.org/4ba9d99d9.pdf
127. Council of the European Union (2002) Contribution of the legal service to the asylum working party on a proposal for a council directive on minimum standards for the qualification and Status of third country nationals and stateless persons as refugees or as persons who otherwise Need protection—articles 1 and 4, council doc 14348/02 of 15 November 2002 (JUR 449, ASILE 67)
128. Storey H (2008) EU refugee qualification directive: a brave new world? Int J Refugee Law 20(1):1–49
129. UNHCR (2007) Asylum in the european union. A study of the implementation of the qualification directive, brussels: UNHCR 2007. Available via http://www.unhcr.org/cgi-bin/texis/vtx/search?page=search&docid=47302b6c2&query=Asylum%20in%20the%20European%20UNion
130. European Commission (2007) Green paper on the future common European asylum system COM (2007) 301 final
131. European Commission (2008) Communication from the commission to the European parliament, the council, the european economic and social committee and the committee of regions, policy plan on asylum—An integrated approach to protection across the EU, COM(2008) 360 final

Chapter 3
Recasting of Asylum Legislation: *Nolumus leges mutari*!

3.1 The Dublin III Regulation: (Still) in Search of a Dialogue Between Burden Sharing, Mutual Trust and Guarantee of Non-refoulement

In June 2013 the Council of Ministers and the European Parliament reached an agreement on the proposed Regulation Recast, which sets out a revised set of rules for the Dublin system on responsibility for asylum-seekers' applications.[1] The Dublin system is a key component of CEAS impacting on Member States' asylum systems but also, and significantly, on the lives of many protection-seekers. As such, its reform has been advocated by many and was much awaited.

The Dublin II Regulation has been widely criticized for failing to adequately protect asylum-seekers' fundamental rights.[2] The responsibility determination rules under the Dublin II Regulation, which linked responsibility for asylum applications to border management by compelling the return of individuals to third countries for the sole reason of having transited through those countries, have ended up overburdening less well-equipped asylum systems as well as creating pressure for irregular or illegal migration within the EU.[3] In particular, the Dublin II Regulation provided that after the consideration of any family links or whether a prior visa or residence permit existed, if it could be established that an asylum-seeker had irregularly entered the border of a Member State by land, sea, or air having come from a third country, the Member State thus entered would be responsible for examining the request for asylum.[4]

Latin adage: 'We do not want the laws to be changed.'

---

[1] See Refs. [1–4].
[2] E.g. Ref. [5–7].
[3] See Ref. [8]; see also Ref. [9].
[4] See Article 10(1) of the Dublin II Regulation, now Article 13(1) Recast.

S. Velluti, *Reforming the Common European Asylum System - Legislative Developments and Judicial Activism of the European Courts*, SpringerBriefs in Law,
DOI: 10.1007/978-3-642-40267-8_3, © The Author(s) 2014

One of the main shortcomings of the Dublin II Regulation, which also characterizes the Dublin Regulation Recast (coined "Dublin III"),[5] was that it was based on the idea that asylum-seekers could rely on equal access to protection and justice in each Member State.[6] In this context, the principle of mutual trust was and remains a fundamental foundational principle underlying the operation of the Dublin system and a key building-block of CEAS,[7] which finds its legal expression in the so-called "presumption of equivalent protection" or more generally a "presumption of safety" among those Member States which are part of the Dublin system.[8] Under the Dublin rules responsibility entails the obligation to take charge of (or to take back) the (failed) asylum-seeker who turns up in a non-responsible state and to examine the claim for asylum. Hence, mutual trust under the Dublin rules concerns the examination of the request for asylum by the other Member State, i.e. the procedure for sorting out whether or not the TCN fulfils the requirements for international protection.[9] It also concerns the treatment of the asylum-seeker during this examination.[10] The justification for mutual trust is enshrined in the Preamble to the Dublin Regulation where it is stated *inter alia* that 'Member States, all respecting the principle of *non-refoulement*, are considered as safe countries for third-country nationals.'[11] The mechanism of mutual recognition as applied in the field of asylum also implies a practice of non-interference with decisions already made on applications for asylum within the EU.[12] This can be seen also in the context of the Asylum Procedures Directive where Member States may declare an application for international protection inadmissible if a decision on the same application has already been made in another Member State.[13] Mutual

[5] For a detailed examination of the Dublin II Regulation's compliance with International Refugee Law, see Ref. [10].

[6] See Ref. [11, 12]; see Ref. [13], at 605–607; Ref. [14], at 971; Ref. [15] at 207.

[7] Battjes defines mutual trust in the Dublin system as follows: 'the assumption that each Member State will treat asylum-seekers and examine their claims in accordance with the relevant rules of national, European and International Law,' see Ref. [16], at p. 9.

[8] See Ref. [17], at 12.

[9] See Battjes (2011), see footnote 7, at pp. 9–10. An exception to mutual trust is represented by the so-called "discretionary clauses" as per Article 17 Recast, discussed further below in this section.

[10] Ibidem, at p. 10.

[11] See Recital 3 of the Dublin Regulation Recast, which states that: 'The European Council, at its special meeting in Tampere on 15 and 16 October 1999, agreed to work towards establishing the CEAS, based on the full and inclusive application of the Geneva Convention Relating to the Status of Refugees of 28 July 1951, as supplemented by the New York Protocol of 31 January 1967 (hereinafter referred to as "the Geneva Convention"), thus ensuring that nobody is sent back to persecution, i.e. maintaining the principle of *non-refoulement*. In this respect, and without the responsibility criteria laid down in this Regulation being affected, Member States, all respecting the principle of *non-refoulement*, are considered as safe countries for third-country nationals.'

[12] See Staffans (2008), see footnote 57 in Chap. 2, at p. 161.

[13] See e.g. Article 33(2)(a) and (d) of the Asylum Procedure Recast Directive.

trust is not absolute and Member States will have to put it aside when this is required to guarantee non-*refoulement*.[14] Nevertheless, mutual trust—and, in particular, mutual recognition of decisions- is a means to ensure the preservation of states' exercise of sovereign powers. In addition, and linked to this, significant differences between Member States as to the level and standard of protection remain a reality of the European asylum landscape.[15] Consequently, great disparities and inequality affecting asylum-seekers as well as certain Member States persist.[16] Studies conducted on the operation of the Dublin system show that it has failed to produce the effects of mutual recognition that it was hoped for and that only a minority of cases that are intended to be transferred through the scheme are actually subject to mutual recognition.[17] In particular, the application of the Dublin system has led to an unequal distribution of displaced persons across Europe and to an increased number of asylum-seekers being returned to Member States on the borders of the enlarged Union, chiefly Central Eastern European countries and Southern Mediterranean countries which have been unable to deal with flows of asylum-seekers,[18] as well as a resort to onward and illegal transit.[19] Hence, under the Dublin II Regulation entry controls have been linked to the allocation of responsibility creating unequal burdens depending on a country's geographical position.[20] Regrettably, this remains unchanged under Dublin III. Arguably, this is contrary to the principle of solidarity and fair sharing of responsibility which according to Article 80 TFEU underlie the adoption and implementation of asylum policies. This state of affairs has had the detrimental effect of leading some

[14] In this sense, see the judgments of *MSS v Belgium and Greece*, Application No. 30696/09, judgment of 21 January 2011 (ECtHR) and Joined Cases C-411/10 and C-493/10 *NS v Secretary of State for the Home Department and ME and Others v Refugee Applications Commissioner and Minister for Justice, Equality and Law Reform*, judgment of the Court (Grand Chamber) of 21 December 2011, nyr, which are examined in much detail in Chap. 4.

[15] In this context it should be noted that the Dublin Regulation not only applies to all Member States, including the UK, which has also opted in Dublin III, Ireland as well as Denmark (by virtue of a treaty between the EU and Denmark), but also to the four non-EU states associated with the EU's "Schengen" rules on abolition of border controls: Norway, Iceland, Switzerland and Liechtenstein. All together and including the newest country to join the EU, namely, Croatia, thirty-two countries are subject to the new rules.

[16] See Ref. [18].

[17] See ECRE (2006), see footnote 6 Ref. [19].

[18] Two countries with well-publicized mal-functioning asylum systems are Greece and Italy. In Greece, problems include many asylum-seekers left in a situation of complete uncertainty as well as poor conditions in detention. Some concerns were raised that this state of affairs could lead to a risk of *refoulement*. However, in practice and in spite of the above problems, it seems that Greece has not been very active in returning asylum-seekers. As to Italy, the problems faced by this country have included the well-known *refoulement* of asylum-seekers trying to reach the island of Lampedusa, and failures to give effective access to the status determination procedures with many protection-seekers being left on the street; for further critical analysis from a human rights perspective, see M. Symes, see footnote 150 in Chap. 2.

[19] See, Ref. [20], at 506.

[20] See Ref. [21], at p. 137; see also Ref. [22].

Member States to adopt restrictive asylum measures thus denying access to a fair and effective asylum procedure. Greece is a case in point.[21] Since early 2004 the Greek authorities have been interrupting the examination of asylum applications for persons who have been returned to Greece under Article 13 of the Dublin II procedure[22] on the basis of Article 2(8) of the Presidential Decree 61/99, which allows the Ministry of Public Order to interrupt the examination of an asylum claim when the applicant "arbitrarily leaves his/her stated place of residence." In practice, the Greek authorities have used this provision to "interrupt" the asylum claims of individuals having transited illegally to other Member States and subsequently have used this as a justification for denying these individuals access to an asylum procedure when returned to Greece under the Dublin Regulation. Even when Greek authorities have accepted responsibility for the asylum claim following a request by another Member State, an interruption decision has been subsequently issued prior to transfer to Greece. Thus, when the applicant was returned to Greece, upon arrival they would be informed of the interruption of the decision, issued with a deportation order and detained prior to expulsion.[23] In addition, there is significant difference in the level of reception conditions in the different Member States.[24]

The Regulation has also been criticized for being an incentive for countries to increasingly resort to using detention as a means to secure Dublin II transfers, discussed further below in this section.[25] Additionally, the operation of the Dublin II Regulation to date has been inefficient, expensive and time-consuming in spite of efficiency being one of its main objectives[26] and it has failed to achieve its goal of reducing the number of multiple applications.[27] In particular, ECRE's findings show that the implementation of the Dublin Regulation has added a lengthy and

[21] The problems concerning the asylum system of Greece and treatment of asylum-seekers is examined further within the jurisprudential analysis of the European Courts, see Chap. 4 in this volume.

[22] Article 13 of the Dublin II Regulation provided that: 'Where no Member State responsible for examining the application for asylum can be designated on the basis of the criteria listed in this Regulation, the first Member State with which the application for asylum was lodged shall be responsible for examining it.' The amended procedure for examining an application for international protection is now to be found in Article 3 of the Recast Regulation. The corresponding provision is now to be found in paragraph 2 which significantly envisages the scenario whereby it may be impossible to transfer an applicant to the Member State primarily designated as responsible because there are substantial grounds for believing that there are systemic flaws in the asylum procedure and in the reception conditions for applicants in that Member State, resulting in a risk of inhuman or degrading treatment within the meaning of Article 4 of the EU Charter.

[23] See Ref. [23]; see also Ref. [24].

[24] See Ref. [25].

[25] See ECRE (2006), see footnote 6.

[26] See Ref. [26], at p. 10.

[27] Ibidem, at p. 11.

cumbersome procedure to the beginning of the asylum process.[28] This lengthy process unnecessarily prolongs the state of uncertainty in which asylum-seekers find themselves as well as delaying refugees' integration in the host country.[29] For these reasons ECRE proposed an alternative system for allocating responsibility for determining an asylum claim which, had it been included in the revised Regulation, would have been conducive to a more efficient and fairer Dublin system.[30] Specifically, the proposal envisaged two criteria: a) the Member State where the asylum-seeker has a family member, provided he or she consents to a transfer to that state; or b) the Member State in which an asylum claim was first lodged, unless there are compelling humanitarian considerations to preclude this. The underlying argument of ECRE's proposal was that the creation and effective operation of CEAS would provide the basis for common asylum procedures and mechanisms for improved quality standards, which in turn would ensure an equivalent treatment of asylum-seekers and refugees throughout the EU and thus avoid the situation whereby certain Member States would be excessively over-burdened.[31] A central component of ECRE's proposal was the development of a series of responsibility sharing and practical co-operation measures aimed at increasing the capacity and efficiency of national asylum systems[32] such as a well-resourced financial burden sharing instrument—based on the costs of hosting and processing asylum claims, which could compensate Member States receiving higher volumes of asylum applications; common co-ordinating bodies and structures to assist overburdened Member States; the setting up of joint responses to major humanitarian crises.[33]

The Dublin Regulation Recast places greater emphasis on the humanitarian dimension of the Dublin system, in line with the objectives of creating CEAS. However, it still fails to sufficiently address the underlying weaknesses of the Dublin system.[34] As mentioned earlier, the main limitations of the Dublin Regulation are associated with the way it has been conceptualized: mainly as an

28 Idem.

29 Ibidem, at p. 26.

30 See Nash and Kok, see footnote 3, at 30.

31 Ibidem, at 31.

32 See Article 80 TFEU which provides that EU (immigration and) asylum policies and their implementation 'shall be governed by the principle of solidarity and fair sharing of responsibility, including its financial implications, between the Member States;' see also Article 67(2) TFEU which provides that EU immigration and asylum policy shall be 'based on solidarity between Member States.'

33 See Article 78(3) TFEU which refers to the issue of an 'emergency situation' constituting a 'sudden inflow' of third-country nationals.

34 See, Ref. [27].

administrative tool for establishing Member States' responsibility for examining asylum claims rather than as a burden-sharing instrument for protecting refugees in the EU,[35] and again Dublin III reproduces this intrinsic logic. In addition, the latter remains premised on the assumption that there is an equal level of standards of protection across the EU failing to take into due consideration the inconsistent level of protection in the Member States. This problem combined with the (untouched) responsibility determination rules for examining an asylum application may hinder the creation of CEAS, which is based on solidarity and integration. In terms of ensuring access to a substantive and fair asylum procedure this is problematic especially when considering that the processing of applications may take several months leaving asylum-seekers waiting in uncertainty for a rather long period of time. The maintenance of the same responsibility determination rules in the Recast Regulation and the lack of harmonization in relation to protection standards—as the European Parliament has observed—may mean that 'the Dublin system [even in its revised form][36] will continue to be unfair both to asylum-seekers and to certain Member States.'[37]

Moving to the key changes introduced by the compromise text of the Dublin Regulation Recast, one of the most significant amendments is the extension of the scope of the Regulation to applicants for all forms of international protection.[38] Moreover, the Regulation also applies to transit zones.[39] With regard to the guarantee of legal safeguards for persons falling within the scope of the Dublin system, there is reference throughout the Recast Regulation to the right to an effective remedy[40] and in this context to free legal assistance and representation. According to Article 27 Recast applicants have the right to judicial review of a transfer decision. In particular, the new provisions included in paragraphs 3 and 4 have added some clarity in relation to the right of appeal or review of a transfer decision, particularly in relation to the issue of whether lodging an appeal has an automatic suspensive effect, which was the subject of much discussion under the

[35] Notably the European Commission said that 'the Dublin system [...] was not devised as a burden sharing instrument,' see Ref. [28], at p. 10. This is also the position of the ECJ, see further in Chap. 4, Sect. 4.3.

[36] Author's addition.

[37] See Ref. [29], (Own Initiative Report).

[38] See Articles 1 and 2(b) and (c) Recast.

[39] See Article 3(1) Recast.

[40] E.g. see Recital 19 (where there is also reference to Article 47 of the EU Charter), Articles 18(2) and 27 Recast.

Dublin II Regulation.[41] Paragraphs 3[42] and 4[43] provide for national law concerning appeals or reviews to envisage one of the following four scenarios, namely, the right for the applicant to remain in the Member State concerned pending the outcome of the decision, automatic suspension of the transfer for a certain reasonable period of time[44] and when such suspension lapses a judicial decision is to follow on whether to grant suspensive effect to an appeal or review, a request within a reasonable period of time to a court or tribunal to suspend the implementation of the transfer decision pending the outcome of his/her appeal or review and that the competent authorities may decide, acting *ex officio*, to suspend the implementation of the transfer decision pending the outcome of the appeal or review. While Article 27 Recast represents a positive step forward from the perspective of the applicant's right to an effective remedy it still leaves Member States with considerable discretion. As a consequence, the procedural guarantees for asylum-seekers against decisions of the Member States remain rather weak in practice.[45] Differences between Member States have not been removed and the

---

[41] E.g. see Case C-19/08 *Migrationsverket v Edgar Petrosian and Others* [2009] ECR I-495, where the ECJ was asked by the referring court to clarify on the meaning of Article 20(1)(d) and (2) of the Dublin II Regulation, fort further analysis of this case, see Ippolito and Velluti (2011), see footnote 55 in Chap. 2, at 35–36.

[42] In particular para 3 provides that: 'For the purposes of appeals against, or reviews of, transfer decisions, Member States shall provide in their national law that: (a) the appeal or review confers upon the person concerned the right to remain in the Member State concerned pending the outcome of the appeal or review; or (b) the transfer is automatically suspended and such suspension lapses after a certain reasonable period of time, during which a court or a tribunal, after a close and rigorous scrutiny, shall have taken a decision whether to grant suspensive effect to an appeal or review; or (c) the person concerned has the opportunity to request within a reasonable period of time a court or tribunal to suspend the implementation of the transfer decision pending the outcome of his or her appeal or review. Member States shall ensure that an effective remedy is in place by suspending the transfer until the decision on the first suspension request is taken. Any decision on whether to suspend the implementation of the transfer decision shall be taken within a reasonable period of time, while permitting a close and rigorous scrutiny of the suspension request. A decision not to suspend the implementation of the transfer decision shall state the reasons on which it is based.'

[43] Paragraph 4 provides that: 'Member States may provide that the competent authorities may decide, acting *ex officio*, to suspend the implementation of the transfer decision pending the outcome of the appeal or review.'

[44] The meaning and interpretation by the ECJ of "reasonable period of time" is examined in much detail in section 3.3, concerning the Asylum Procedures Directive, further below.

[45] The right to an effective remedy does not only require the *existence* but also *accessibility* of such remedy for an individual. Any limitations imposed by the Member States must be necessary to pursue a legitimate aim and proportionate to the aim it purports to achieve, and must no impair the very essence of the right of access to an effective remedy. In this sense, see *Shamayev and Others v Georgia and Russia*, Application No. 36378/02, judgment of 12 April 2005, para 447, where the ECtHR stated that the exercise of the remedy must not be unjustifiably hindered by the acts or omissions of the authorities of the respondent state, and similarly in *Čonka* the ECtHR stated that the circumstances voluntarily created by the authorities must be such as to afford applicants a realistic possibility of using the remedy, see *Čonka v Belgium*, Application No. 51524/99, para 46.

main objective of having a harmonized Dublin system remains far from being achieved. Arguably, having a single provision requiring Member States to have national laws in place granting automatic suspensive effect to applicants' appeals, in combination with a full examination of the grounds of an appeal in a single hearing, would have ensured an expedited procedure, speed the final assessment of the protection claim, reduce overall judicial burdens, and decrease costs to Member States, which are required to provide legal representation for both sides.[46]

As to the suspension of transfers, the Commission's Recast proposal contained a procedure which would have allowed the Commission—on its own initiative or on the initiative of another Member State—to suspend Dublin transfers to a Member State when 'circumstances prevailing in the Member State concerned may lead to a level of protection for applicants for international protection which is not in conformity with Community legislation, in particular with the Reception Conditions Directive and the Asylum Procedures Directive.'[47] According to the proposal, the Commission would have based a decision to suspend transfers on 'an examination of all the relevant circumstances prevailing in the Member State,' state the reasons for the decision, and specify among other things 'any particular conditions attached to such suspension.' The proposed Article 31 stated that the Commission would have to determine whether the grounds for the suspension persisted after a 6-months period.[48] ECRE suggested to strengthen monitoring and accountability by way of developing fourty benchmarks to assess progress, requiring the Member State concerned to report progress on the basis of those benchmarks within 6 months.[49] ECRE also proposed to amend this provision by including a reference to the fact that a failure to act to rectify the issues identified by the Commission would have consequences such as, for example, the initiation of infringement proceedings by the Commission, in order to prevent that suspensions would not be unduly prolonged, and to avoid any risk that the suspension may end up having detrimental effects on the applicants.[50] The proposal further provided that a Member State could request the Commission to temporarily suspend incoming Dublin II transfers when faced with 'a particularly urgent situation which places an exceptionally heavy burden on its reception capacities, asylum system or infrastructure, and when the transfer of applicants for international protection in accordance with this Regulation to that Member State could add to that burden.'[51]

The Commission proposal on the above "suspension mechanism," as amended by the European Parliament,[52] was met with opposition from the Council.[53]

---

[46] See Nash and Kok, see footnote 3, at 7.

[47] See Article 31(2–3) of the Recast Proposal.

[48] See Article 31(8) of the Recast Proposal.

[49] See Nash and Kok, see footnote 3, at 11.

[50] Idem.

[51] See Article 31(1) of the Recast Proposal.

[52] See Ref. [30].

[53] See Ref. [31].

A so-called "early warning system" has replaced the Commission's proposed suspension mechanism, which envisages an important role for EASO and it enables the Commission to make recommendations to a Member State with problems in its asylum system, inviting it to draw up a "preventive action plan."[54] The wording of Article 33 in the final compromise text clearly indicates that it is left to the discretion of the Member State concerned. In the case of a lack of improvement the Commission in cooperation with the Member State in question may then elaborate a "crisis management action plan" and the said Member State would then have to submit regular reports on the implementation of these plans.[55] In addition, paragraph 4 of Article 33 also envisages a significant role for the Council as it states that during the entire process for early warning, preparedness and crisis management the Council shall closely monitor the situation and may request further information and provide political guidance, in particular as regards the urgency and severity of the situation and thus the need for a Member State to draw up either a "preventive action plan" or, if necessary, a "crisis management action plan." There is also the possibility for an involvement of the European Parliament in relation to discussing and providing guidance with the Council on any solidarity measures as they deem appropriate. Overall, the said "early warning mechanism" is a more nuanced measure than the one proposed by the Commission, which does not provide for any specific time-frame and is open to flexibility and discretion. Moreover, the involvement of so many EU Institutions and the different stages envisaged also make it a rather hefty and lengthy process. Hence, once again not only the fundamental rights of a protection-seeker are in jeopardy but the objective of securing efficiency is also seriously undermined.

The Recast Directive also introduces some safeguards against the arbitrary or excessive use of detention in the context of the procedure to transfer an asylum-seeker or an applicant for subsidiary protection to the responsible Member State as asylum-seekers are frequently detained in the context of these procedures.[56] First, Article 28(1) Recast refers to the principle contained in the Asylum Procedures Directive that individuals should not be detained exclusively on the basis that they are seeking international protection.[57] In addition, Article 28(2) Recast only allows detention in cases where there is a significant risk of absconding, on the basis of an

---

[54] See Council of the European Union (2013), Position of the Council at first reading with a view to the adoption of a Regulation of the European Parliament and of the Council establishing the criteria and mechanisms for determining the Member State responsible for examining an application for international protection lodged in one of the Member States by a third-country national or a stateless person (recast), Brussels 31 May 2013, Doc No. 15605/2/12 REV 2, Article 33; see also Ref. [32].

[55] See Article 33(3) Recast.

[56] This would be in line with the ECtHR's jurisprudence, see *Amuur v. France,* ECHR (1996), Application No. 19776/92, para 53, where the Court stated that 'there must be adequate legal protection in domestic law against arbitrary interferences by public authorities with the rights safeguarded by the Convention.'

[57] See Article 26(1) of the Recast Asylum Procedures Directive.

individual assessment of each case and only in so far as detention is proportional and other less coercive measures cannot be applied effectively. Alternatives to detention, which equally prevent the risk of absconding, are for example: regular reporting to the authorities, the deposit of a financial guarantee, an obligation to stay at a designated place. However, Article 2(n) Recast, which defines the "risk of absconding,"[58] does not include a list of objective criteria that Member States may use in establishing such a risk and thus Member States may interpret such as a provision at their own discretion. Hence, while this provision may represent an improvement in terms of applicants' legal safeguards, the risk of arbitrary detention nonetheless remains. The detention should be for the shortest period possible and for a period of time reasonably necessary to fulfil the required administrative procedures for carrying out a transfer.[59] While this constitutes an improvement from the perspective of asylum-seekers' procedural guarantees, an important safeguard permitting the use of detention only after the notification of the decision to transfer to the applicant and only after the agreement of the requested Member State with the transfer, has been removed in the final compromise text.[60] Nevertheless, the Council has maintained in the text other Commission's proposals concerning detention conditions and related guarantees and there is also reference to Article 31 of the Geneva Convention obligations.[61] Significantly, Article 28(4) states that as regards the detention conditions and the guarantees applicable to persons detained, in order to secure the transfer procedures to the Member State responsible, Articles 9, 10 and 11 of the Reception Conditions Directive shall apply. Moreover, in Recital 11 there is a broader reference to Reception Conditions Directive clearly stating that this Directive also applies to asylum-seekers under the Dublin procedure.[62]

Other important amendments emphasizing a stronger humanitarian perspective concern the definition of family members and family unification. The amendments also expand the definition of "family members" as the definition no longer encompasses only family links that already existed in the country of origin.

---

[58] See Article 2(n) Recast, which provides that: '"risk of absconding" means the existence of reasons in an individual case, which are based on objective criteria defined by law, to believe that an applicant or a third-country national or a stateless person who is subject to a transfer procedure may abscond.'

[59] See Article 28(3) Recast.

[60] See Article 27(4) Recast.

[61] See Council of the European Union (2013a), see footnote 1, Recital 20 and Article 28.

[62] See Case C-179/11, *CIMADE and GISTI v. Ministry of the Interior* lodged on 18 April 2011, pending, where the French Council of State has requested a preliminary ruling from the ECJ concerning the applicability of the Reception Conditions Directive to asylum-seekers awaiting the determination of the State responsible for examining their asylum claims under the Dublin II Regulation; see also Case C-179/11 Opinion of the Advocate-General Sharpston delivered on 15 May 2012 for whom, on the basis of a combined reading of Articles 1 (on human dignity) and 18 (on the right of asylum) of the EU Charter and in the light of the Tampere Conclusions and the objectives of CEAS, the answer is clearly in the affirmative; for further commentary and analysis also in relation to and in the light of international human rights instruments see Ref. [33].

Although the meaning of "family members" in Article 2(g) refers to a family that already existed in the country of origin, references in other Articles of the Recast Directive also include "or any other family relations" or "regardless of whether the family was previously formed in the country of origin."[63] In relation to family unification, the Recast Directive clearly includes family unification in the hierarchy of criteria by moving part of the current humanitarian clause to the hierarchy. Specifically, Member States would be required to reunite unaccompanied minors or dependant relatives with other relatives present in Member States.[64] Moreover, in addition to prioritizing the unification of unaccompanied minors with relatives in the responsibility criteria, the Recast Directive introduces general safeguards for children and specifies that the best interests of the child are a primary consideration therefore requiring that Member States should trace all relatives of an unaccompanied minor in any Member State.[65] In addition, national authorities would be required to receive training concerning the specific needs of minors.[66] The Recast merges the remainder of the humanitarian clause with the sovereignty clause as discretionary clauses.[67] Hence, a transfer under the discretionary clauses would continue to depend on the willingness of the receiving Member State.

By way of conclusion, the foregoing analysis and the findings therein seem to suggest that the recasting process of the Dublin system has undergone various and difficult stages in which a more rights-based approach in favour of asylum-seekers—now clearly included in comparison with the Dublin II Regulation-remains nevertheless in tension with a security paradigm aimed at preserving Member States' prerogatives. Hence, the procedural safeguards inserted in the final compromise text still fail to amount to a sufficiently robust guarantee of *non-refoulement*.

[63] See Recitals 17 and 18, Articles 4(1)(c), 7(3), 9, 31(2)(b) and 34(2)(a) Recast.

[64] See Articles 6(4) and 8 Recast.

[65] See Recitals 13 where there is explicit reference to the 1989 UN Convention on the Rights of the Child, 16 and 24, Article 6 Recast; see also Case C-648/11, *MA, BT, DA v Secretary of State for the Home Department*, Judgment of 6 June 2013, where the ECJ held that Article 6(2) of the Dublin Regulation must be interpreted as meaning that, in circumstances where an unaccompanied minor who does not have relatives legally residing in the EU, has lodged asylum applications in more than one Member State, shall remain in the country where their most recent asylum application was lodged and that Member State shall take responsibility for the examination (at para 66). Two aspects of the Court's ruling are particularly noteworthy. First, the reference to unaccompanied minors as a being a category of particularly vulnerable persons (at para 55) and, second, the emphasis on the best interest of the child in all actions relating to him/her, whether taken by a public authority or private institutions, as per Article 24(2) of the EU Charter (at para 57), which consequently require that procedures for determining the Member State responsible are not unnecessarily prolonged and that unaccompanied minors have prompt access to the procedures for determining refugee status (at para 61).

[66] See Article 6(4), subpara 3 Recast.

[67] See Article 17 Recast.

3.2 The New Qualification Directive: Who is the New Refugee?

The Qualification Directive rests at the centre of EU refugee law, defining the standards of who qualifies for international protection.[68] The original Qualification Directive significantly expanded the wording of Article 1A of the Geneva Convention and articulated the elements of the refugee definition more precisely.[69] Nevertheless, it was not devoid of significant omissions and derogations allowing Member States to have different recognition status of asylum-seekers across the EU.[70] With regard to the definition of "beneficiaries" of international protection, the Qualification Directive apparently resulted in a significant degree of harmonization of the interpretation of the Geneva Convention refugee definition, as well the criteria for granting subsidiary protection in accordance with international human rights obligations.[71] However, the original Qualification Directive also allowed for certain "optional mechanisms and exclusive procedures"[72] that deviated from the general standards. In particular, Member States were given the option to exclude persons falling within the harmonized Geneva Convention refugee definition from being granted EU refugee status under security-related criteria which in practice constituted exclusion grounds in addition to, and therefore at variance with, the Geneva Convention.[73] Other ambiguities to be found in the Qualification Directive concerned the standards for the assessment of facts that left quite a wide margin of discretion to national authorities as well as the provision regarding the recognition of refugee status *sur place* which rather than eliminating differences of interpretation and application in the Member States seemed to permit diverging national interpretations and internal inconsistency.[74] The approach of the Directive to international protection needs *sur place* remains ambivalent. In particular, as Da Lomba notes the Directive seems to establish a hierarchy between asylum claims *sur place* based on events that occurred in the country of origin post-departure and claims that rely on actions engaged in since leaving that country.[75] While the former are looked upon favourably, the latter are

---

[68] See Ref. [34].

[69] See Ref. [35], at 97.

[70] For critical academic commentary and policy analysis papers, see H. Battjes (2006), see footnote 55 in Chap. 2, pp. 219–274; Gilbert (2004), see footnote 6, Refs. [36–40]; H. Storey (2008), see footnote 162 in Chap. 2; see also See Refs. [41, 42].

[71] See Articles 4–8 of the 2004 Qualification Directive (general standards), Articles 9–14 (refugee status) and Articles 15–19 (subsidiary protection).

[72] See Vedsted-Hansen (2011), see footnote 66 in Chap. 2.

[73] See Articles 14(4) and (5); Article 12 (grounds for exclusion) of the 2004 Qualification Directive which are based for the most part on Article 1 D, E and F of the Geneva Convention.

[74] See specifically Article 5(2) and (3) of the 2004 Qualification Directive; see Da Lomba (2011), see footnote 70.

[75] Ibidem, at p. 45.

suspected of being manufactured. Asylum claims *sur place* must be assessed on the same basis as other claims for refugee status.[76] However, there is reluctance to do so in respect of claims that are based on post-departure activity the fear being abuse of the asylum process.[77] Article 5(3) of the Qualification Directive singled out manufactured subsequent applications for refugee status and indirectly relied on the idea of bad faith as a bar to refugee status.[78] On the other hand, Article 4(3)(d) as well as Article 20(6) and (7) made clear that international protection status could be granted to persons who had manufactured their need for international protection, although the latter foresaw the imposition of reductions of benefits of a punitive nature for those who had been granted protection on the basis of manufactured claims. Such reductions may engage Member States' obligations under the Geneva Convention and international human rights instruments.[79] Hence, 'such curtailments of rights cannot fall short of the minimum standards set out in the 1951 Convention nor can they fall below the Member States' international human rights obligations.'[80] It follows that only those rights not guaranteed in binding international instruments could potentially be limited.[81] It should be noted that the Geneva Convention does not provide for punitive sanctions for asylum-seekers who engaged in activity *sur place* for the sole purpose of gaining refugee status and the principle of non-discrimination is a basic principle of international refugee law.[82]

The 2004 Qualification Directive also included optional provisions in relation to "protection standards" for persons who have been granted protection under the Directive. First, it allowed for the reduction of standards for those refugees and subsidiary protection beneficiaries whose status was deemed to have been obtained on the basis of activities engaged in 'for the sole or main purpose of creating the necessary conditions for being recognized' as a refugee or a person eligible for subsidiary protection. Indeed, despite the condition that such reduction had to be within the limits set by the Refugee Convention and other international obligations the Directive clearly deferred important aspects of the issue to the Member States.[83] In addition, there was also significant deference to Member States as regards the application of differential standards for subsidiary protection beneficiaries in comparison with Geneva Convention refugees. The standard concerning

---

[76] See Ref. [43].

[77] See Ref. [44], at p. 200; see also Ref. [45].

[78] *Contra*, the principle of good faith is a principle of public international law which concerns the conduct of the parties which have bound themselves by an international treaty and does not bind individuals, see H. Lambert (2006), see footnote 70, at 172.

[79] See H. Battjes (2006), see footnote 55 in Chap. 2, at p. 485; see also [46], at 1538, for whom these reductions may be in line with international human rights law although they do evoke and cast suspicion on the protection-seeker and discredit the assessment for the need of protection.

[80] See Da Lomba (2011), see footnote 70, at p. 60.

[81] Ibidem, at p. 61.

[82] See Article 3 of the Geneva Convention.

[83] See Article 20(6) and (7) of the 2004 Qualification Directive.

access to employment is a case in point. In particular, while refugees could be authorized to engage in employed or self-employed activities immediately after their refugee status was granted to them,[84] that right was significantly qualified for beneficiaries of subsidiary protection as the 'situation of the labour market' could be taken into account, including for possible prioritization of access to employment for a limited period of time' which was to be determined in accordance with national law; and subsidiary protection beneficiaries had to have access to a post for which they had received an offer 'in accordance with national rules on prioritization in the labour market.'[85] Further differentiation was permitted on the right of subsidiary protection beneficiaries to social welfare and health care, both of which could be limited to 'core benefits' that would then have to be provided at the same levels and under the same eligibility conditions as nationals.[86] Another limitation of the original Qualification Directive, that many have raised as being particularly problematic, was the personal scope of the refugee definition contained in the Directive. The definition was confined to TCNs and stateless persons which was inconsistent with the Geneva Convention definition. This limitation was rooted in old Article 63(1)(c) EC, i.e. the legal basis for adopting the Directive. The foregoing analysis seems to suggest that while the 2004 Qualification Directive emphatically affirmed the Geneva Convention as the cornerstone of refugee protection, the obligations set out in the Convention were perceived as constraints.[87]

In 2009 the European Commission issued a proposal to recast the Directive.[88] The Recast proposal aimed at addressing inconsistencies, achieving a higher level of harmonization and ensuring coherence with the jurisprudence of the ECJ and the ECtHR.[89] Negotiations between the European Parliament and the Council led to the adoption of the Recast Directive in December 2011.[90] Hence, of the "core" EU asylum Directives, this is the first major piece of legislation to have been adopted under the co-decision procedure.[91] Not only has the legal regime changed

---

[84] See Article 26(1) of the 2004 Qualification Directive.

[85] See Article 26(3) of the 2004 Qualification Directive.

[86] See Article 28(2) and 29(2) of the 2004 Qualification Directive. For a definition of 'core benefits' see Recital 34 of the Preamble to the 2004 Qualification Directive which states that the former cover 'at least minimum income support, assistance in case of illness, pregnancy and parental assistance, in so far as they are granted to nationals according to Member States' legislation.

[87] See Da Lomba (2011), see footnote 70, at p. 62.

[88] See European Commission (2009), see footnote 81 in Chap. 2.

[89] See European Commission (2009), Explanatory Memorandum to the 2009 Qualification Recast Proposal, at pp. 2–4.

[90] See Ref. [47].

[91] Special opt-out arrangements apply to Ireland and the UK which decided not to opt into the Recast Directive. These two Member States continue to be bound by the provisions of the 2004 version of the Directive, see Recital 50 of Directive 2011/95/EU.

since the adoption of the original Qualification Directive, but the new Qualification Directive has seen several significant changes from the original.

The new Qualification Directive contains some visible improvements. First, there is greater acknowledgment of gender-specific forms of persecution and the inclusion of gender identity as a potential ground for protection.[92] It also includes a clear commitment to take the best interest of the child into account[93] and there is a broader notion of "family members" so as to include married minor children among the beneficiaries of international protection, which puts the Qualification Directive better in line with the international obligations deriving from the 1989 United Nations Convention on the Rights of the Child as well as with the ECtHR case-law. However, the proviso that family ties have to exist already in the country of origin remains.[94] In addition, it approximates the content of rights granted to beneficiaries of subsidiary protection and refugees in many areas such as access to employment and to health care.[95]

Nevertheless, certain significant gaps and inconsistencies remain. The new Directive does not broaden the personal scope of the Directive and continues to provide that only "third-country nationals and stateless persons" can qualify as refugees or beneficiaries of subsidiary protection.[96] A broadening of the personal scope would have ensured a closer alignment with the Geneva Convention and in particular with the principle of non-discrimination on grounds of nationality.[97] In addition, it does not address the concerns raised in relation to the grounds for "serious harm" necessary for being eligible for subsidiary protection in Article 15(c) and the apparent "oxymoron" created by the uncomfortable pairing of "indiscriminate violence" and "individual threat" in the same provision. In particular, despite the lack of clarity and ambiguity of the disposition, the notion of

[92] See Recital 30 of the 2011 Qualification Directive which states that: 'It is equally necessary to introduce a common concept of the persecution ground "membership of a particular social group." For the purposes of defining a particular social group, issues arising from an applicant's gender, including gender identity and sexual orientation, which may be related to certain legal traditions and customs, resulting in for example genital mutilation, forced sterilisation or forced abortion, should be given due consideration in so far as they are related to the applicant's well-founded fear of persecution,' Article 4(3)(c) (assessment of an application for international protection), Article 9(2)(f) (acts of persecution), Article 10(1)(d), final subpara. In relation to the latter provision, Ippolito argues that better compliance would have been achieved by explicitly providing that the criteria in Article 10(1)(d) for determining the concept of "membership of a particular social group" have to be considered as alternative and not cumulative requirements, see Ippolito and Velluti (2011), see footnote 55 in Chap. 2, at 37.

[93] See Recitals 18, 19 and 38, Article 20(5) (general rules on the content of international protection), Article 31(4)(5) (unaccompanied minors), of the 2011 Qualification Directive.

[94] See Article 2(j) of the 2011 Qualification Directive.

[95] This is mostly evident in Chapter VII on the content of international protection. In some instances, however, there are still differences, see e.g. Article 24 of the 2011 Qualification Directive on residence permits.

[96] See e.g. Articles 1 and 2 of the 2011 Qualification Directive.

[97] See Article 3 of the Geneva Convention.

"individual threat" provided in Article 15(c) has been left untouched, which makes it difficult to include in the concept of "protection" all categories of persons in need of "protection" but who do not qualify as refugees.[98] Even though the provision includes two contradictory concepts, that of "indiscriminate violence" and "individual threat", which AG Maduro has described as "*prima facie* irreconcilable",[99] the European Commission, as explained in the Impact Assessment of the Proposal,[100] considers that the jurisprudence of the ECJ removes any doubts as to the interpretation of the term "individual," specifically in relation to whether Article 15(c) requires a higher level of proof than Article 15(a) and (b), and whether the provision's scope is broader than that of Article 3 ECHR. In *Elgafaji* the ECJ interpreted the concept of "individual threat" quite broadly[101] and in so doing it mitigated the potential negative effects of Recital 34 of the Directive.[102] In spite of this broad approach, the Court has defined the existence of such a threat as exceptional and thus it permits national courts to interpret the requirement imposed by Article 15 in an excessively narrow sense.[103]

Moreover, as explained by Eaton[104] the definition of "protection" has been modified; substituting the two-part Article 8 definition found in the original Directive for three definitions, two contained in 8(1)(a) and one in 8(1)(b). The Recast Article 8(1)(a) definition remains largely unchanged from the original, which referred to a denial of status based on no well-founded fear or no risk of serious harm, while the recast 8(1)(b) definition simply refers back to the Article 7 definition of protection. The provisions contained in Article 8(1)(a) and 8(1)(b) are disjunctive, suggesting a choice of standards between (a) or (b).[105] The Recast seems to allow a choice between 8(1)(a) and 8(1)(b) standards, which would seem to discourage harmonization, as status determination authorities, motivated by judicial conservatism or simple inertia, can simply opt for the original definition under which Member States have operated since 2004 and which lives on in Article 8(1)(a), rendering 8(1)(b) effectively a dead letter.[106] Additionally—as explained further below- the Recast does little to cure longstanding problems with the internal protection alternative (IPA) in terms of its accordance with international refugee law. Article 8 allows Member States to consider IPA as 'part of the assessment of the application for international protection.' Despite the fact that

98 While Article 15(a) is based on the 6th and 13th Protocol of the ECHR and Article 15(b) may be considered an exact copy of Article 3 ECHR. Article 15(c) covers broad situations of general violence, a feature which is not covered explicitly in the provisions of the ECHR.

99 See AG Maduro Opinion in C-465/07 *Elgafaji v. Staatssecretaris van Justitie* [2009] ECR I-921, para 31.

100 See Ref. [48].

101 See Case C-465/07 *Elgafaji v. Staatssecretaris van Justitie* [2009] ECR I-921, para 43.

102 See Ippolito commentary in Ippolito and Velluti (2011), see footnote 55 in Chap. 2, at 43.

103 Ibidem, at 44.

104 See Eaton (2012), see footnote 68.

105 See Eaton (2012), see footnote 68, at 766.

106 Idem.

scholars have cautioned against linking the IPA determination to the well-founded fear clause, due to the risk that this allows IPA to be used as a "threshold condition" for accessing international protection,[107] the Qualification Directive (both the original Article 8 and the Recast Article 8(1)(a)) seems to do exactly this. The potential risk is that the *initial* refugee status determination could be denied on the grounds of a protection alternative. This kind of "short cut" to status denial based on IPA can skip the critical analysis of the conditions that lead to the applicant fleeing in the first place.[108] Further, such use of the IPA is contrary to UNCHR's position.[109]

To sum up, there are inconsistencies in applying the IPA analysis within Europe and by simply adding a new test in the Recast Qualification Directive it seems unlikely that it will succeed in generating greater harmonization in the EU.

3.3 The Recasting of the Asylum Procedures Directive: Effective, Fair…or Neither?

Among the key legislative measures in the field of asylum, the Asylum Procedures Directive is probably the one that best illustrates the underlying tensions in this area and thus the difficulties encountered in reaching an agreement on its exact content. To date, its interpretation and application has been complicated by a number of incongruities and inconsistencies related to the troublesome legislative history of the Directive.[110] This state of affairs is further confirmed by the European Commission's adoption of a new Recast Proposal in 2011[111] amending the first Recast Proposal of 2009.[112] In June 2013, the European Parliament in plenary session endorsed the draft of the Council of Ministers on the recasting of the Asylum Procedures Directive and at the time of writing there is an agreed finalized text.[113] While retaining some elements of the 2009 recast, the Amended draft introduces significant changes to accommodate concerns expressed by the Council of Ministers and individual Member States in relation to abuses of national asylum systems and cost-effective procedures. In general terms, the new text constitutes a weak attempt to strike a balance between Member States' practical requirements and those stemming from international law and the case law of the ECJ and the

[107] See Eaton (2012), see footnote 68, who also examines extensively academic commentary on this issue.

[108] See Ref. [49], at p. 371.

[109] See Ref. [50].

[110] See Ref. [51], at pp. 1257–1258.

[111] See Ref. [52].

[112] See Ref. [53]. The UK and Ireland have opted out of the recast Directive.

[113] See Refs. [54–56]; for the agreed text visit: www.statewatch.org/news/2013/mar/eu-council-procedures-7695-13.pdf.

ECtHR. The final compromise text contains a number of strengthened procedural guarantees. However, it illustrates the difficulty of harmonizing administrative procedures rooted in diverging and longstanding national legal traditions.[114] While the final text may be said to represent a positive step towards establishing common procedures for the granting or withdrawing of international protection as per Article 78 (2)(d) TFEU, its provisions overall are insufficient for establishing *common procedures* for the granting or withdrawing of a '*uniform status* [...] *valid throughout the Union*'[115] because of the many derogations that it still permits. In its comments on the 2011 amended recast proposal UNHRC argues that while the use of an instrument like a Directive was congruous for the achievement of "minimum standards," namely the declared purpose of the first phase of CEAS, the establishment of "common procedures" and of a "uniform status of asylum valid throughout the Union" requires the use of a Regulation which has direct effect and is directly applicable in the Member States; not a legislative instrument such as the Directive which allows for the adoption of divergent national measures.[116]

Among the positive changes there is the procedural guarantee that all asylum-seekers will now, in principle, have the right to be heard in an interview and to submit comments and clarifications after the interview and before a decision is taken on their claim.[117] Article 31(5)(b) Recast includes the possibility for Member States to prioritize the examination of an application 'where the applicant is vulnerable within the meaning of Article 22 of the Reception Directive or in need of special procedural guarantees, in particular unaccompanied minors.'

In addition, asylum-seekers in an accelerated procedure must now at least be given the opportunity to request in court to stay in the territory while they appeal against a negative decision on their case.[118] Another positive change is the modified definition of "applicant in need of special procedural guarantees" inserted in the Directive[119] and the explicit reference to the fact that this particular category of applicants should be provided with adequate support, including sufficient time, in order to create the conditions necessary for an effective access to procedures and presenting the elements needed to substantiate the application for international protection. In the Commission's 2011 amended recast proposal,

---

[114] For critical academic commentary, see in particular Costello (2005), see footnote 78 in Chap. 2; J. Vedsted-Hansen (2011), see footnote 66 in Chap. 2.

[115] See Article 78 (2)(a) TFEU, emphasis added; see also Article 78 (2) (b) TFEU and Article 1 Recast.

[116] See Ref. [57], p. 5.

[117] See Articles 14–17 Recast.

[118] See Article 46(6), (7)(a), (8) Recast.

[119] See Recital 23 which includes in this category an applicant 'who due to *inter alia* their age, gender, sexual orientation, gender identity, disability, serious illness, mental disorders or consequences of torture, rape or other serious forms of psychological, physical or sexual violence' may be in need of special procedural guarantees.

Article 2(d)[120] included a clear definition of such applicants which disappointingly is not reproduced in the compromise text. The new provision merely refers to 'an applicant whose ability to benefit from the rights and comply with the obligations provided for in this Directive is limited due to *individual circumstances*.'[121] The revised definition, along with the new formulation of Article 24 Recast, does not create a new status category and a case-by-case assessment is necessary to establish whether and applicant falls within the scope of the above definition.[122] As to accelerated procedures, according to Article 24(3) Recast applicants in need of special procedural guarantees cannot be subject to them, this being in line with paragraph 1 of the same Article which provides for sufficient time and relevant support to present the elements of their application.

This positive development, however, is in contrast with other aspects which arguably reduce procedural safeguards. In particular, with regard to vulnerable groups such as unaccompanied children and victims of torture, there will be no exemption from accelerated and border procedures.[123] Despite the fact that establishing stronger guarantees for vulnerable asylum-seekers was one of the key objectives of the asylum package, the standards have been watered down throughout the process. In addition, Article 25(4) Recast does not foresee the provision of legal assistance free of charge to unaccompanied minors at first instance. However, in light of the particular vulnerability of unaccompanied minors, the possibility of limiting free assistance at first instance to the provision of legal information on the procedure and to the explanation of reasons in fact and in law, in the case of a negative decision, is disconcerting. Free legal assistance in first instance provided to unaccompanied minors should have also encompassed the preparation of procedural documents and legal representation, including participation in the personal interview.[124] More generally, no real progress has been made in strengthening the guarantees for ensuring that asylum-seekers have access to legal assistance in practice.[125] This limitation is in stark contrast with the provisions included to address Member States' concerns of preventing misuse of asylum procedures. For instance, procedures have been simplified,[126] training for

[120] This was a provision requested by the European Parliament and within the Council of Ministers it was jointly requested by the German, French and United Kingdom, see Refs. [58, 59].

[121] Emphasis added.

[122] See UNHCR (2012), see footnote 116, p. 6.

[123] See Article 24(3) subpara 2 Recast in relation to applicants in need of special procedural guarantees, which as worded does not exclude the possibility that they can be applied, and Article 25(6)(a) and (b) in relation to unaccompanied minors.

[124] See UNHCR (2012), see footnote 116, p. 21.

[125] See provisions in Articles 20–23 Recast, where there is a prevalence of the use of the term "may" giving Member States a fairly wide margin of discretion and thus allowing for differences between the Member States.

[126] E.g. the "Specific procedures" in Article 24 Recast has been repealed.

the determining authority is envisaged[127] and obligations for applicants for international protection to cooperate with the competent authority have been strengthened.[128] In addition, the new Directive envisages the possibility of considering fraudulent applications in accelerated procedures and for declaring them manifestly unfounded.[129]

With regard to time limits for examination procedures, the new rules introduce a standard six-month deadline for Member States to decide on asylum applications.[130] They can postpone their decisions only for a further nine months, in three limited and now well-defined cases.[131] However, with regard to the second scenario, namely, a large number of third country nationals or stateless persons simultaneously requesting international protection, no definition is provided and there is a risk of unjustified prolongation of procedures, with associated costs and uncertainties for all concerned. Member States may also postpone starting the procedure if there is a "temporarily uncertain situation" in the country of origin.[132] In such cases national authorities would have to review their situation assessment at least every six months. In any event, it is provided that Member States will have to conclude the procedure within a maximum time-limit of twenty-one months from the lodging of the application. The insertion of this derogation is problematic and it is at variance with international refugee law and EU law. It is not in line with the case-law of the ECJ and could trigger increased costs in procedures and reception entitlements, which Member States are bound to continue to afford for the duration of the "uncertain" situation.[133] Efficient and fair procedures for the determination of international protection need to be within a reasonable time.[134]

[127] See Article 4(3) Recast. The list of subjects to be included in the mandatory training for the determining authority has been linked to the list of subjects in Article 6(4) of the Regulation establishing EASO (Regulation 439/2010). Unlike the 2009 recast, however, the list does not include evidence assessment, which is one of the modules of the European Asylum Curriculum (EAC) and is part of the training established and managed by EASO and Member States are only required to 'take into account' the EAC and the training established by EASO. Divergent outcomes are thus still possible and do not serve the purpose of harmonization.

[128] See Article 13(1) Recast.

[129] See 31(6)(e) Recast.

[130] See Article 31(2) Recast.

[131] See Article 31(3) Recast.

[132] See Article 31(3), last indent, Recast.

[133] See UNHCR (2012), see footnote 116, p. 24.

[134] E.g. see C-327/02, *Panayotova and others v. Minister voor Vreemdelingenzaken en Integratie,* ECR [2004] I-11055; see also C-432/05 *Unibet (London) Ltd and Unibet (International) Ltd v Justitiekanslern* ECR [2007] I-2271, where the Court said that 'detailed procedural rules governing actions for safeguarding an individual's rights under Community law [...] must not render practically impossible or excessively difficult the exercise of rights conferred by Community law (principle of effectiveness)' (para 43) and Case C-506/04, *Wilson v Conseil de l'ordre des Avocats du Barreau de Luxembourg* ECR [2006] I-8613, where the Court held that [a provision of a Directive] 'requires actual access within a reasonable period [...] to a court or tribunal as defined by Community law, which is competent to give a ruling on both fact and law' (para 60); see also Article 47 of the EU Charter.

Arguably, such a prolonged postponement of the enjoyment of the right to asylum could potentially breach Article 18 of the EU Charter which provides that the right to asylum shall be guaranteed in accordance with the Geneva Convention. Both this Convention and EU asylum law envisage scenarios where an "uncertain situation" in the country of origin ends. When the circumstances in connection with which the applicant has been granted international protection have ceased to exist, cessation or withdrawal of his/her status can be invoked.[135] Rather than postponing the conclusion of the procedure, Member States should process applications, grant international protection where required and make use of EU asylum rules to withdraw international protection when the circumstances in connection with which the applicant has been granted international protection cease to exist.

With regard to accelerated procedures,[136] a wide range of safeguards has been included for claims that are channelled through such procedures. These include: no omission of the personal interview in such cases,[137] reasonable time limits for the adoption of the decision and an adequate and complete examination, including of manifestly unfounded claims,[138] reasonable time limits for appeal,[139] and the possibility to ask for the suspensive effect of an appeal.[140] With regard to border claims, Article 4(2) Recast provides that only the designated determining authority shall have the prerogative to examine the claim or to interview the applicant at the border. Moreover, according to Article 31(6)(e) Recast, the examination of a claim may be accelerated if the 'applicant has made clearly false or obviously improbable representations which contradict sufficiently verified country of origin information, thus making his/her claim clearly unconvincing' in relation to whether she/he qualifies for international protection. UNHCR criticizes the insertion of the term "improbable representations" as it does not follow necessarily that his/her claim is clearly abusive, fraudulent or unfounded.[141] In addition, Article 31(6)(g) Recast allows for an examination of a claim to be accelerated if 'the applicant may for serious reasons be considered a danger to the national security or public order of the Member State, or the applicant has been forcibly expelled for serious

[135] See Ref. [60]; see also Articles 11 and 12 of the Qualification Directive and Articles 44 and 45 of the Asylum Procedures Directive; see also Joined Cases C-175/08, C-176/08, C-178/08 and C-179/08 *Aydin Salahadin Abdulla and Others v Bundesrepublik Deutschland* ECR [2010] I-01493, on cessation and revocation of refugee status (Article 11 of the Qualification Directive), Case C-31/09 *Nawras Bolbol v Bevándorlási és Állampolgársági Hivatal* ECR [2010] I-05539 and Joined Cases C-57/09 and C-101/09 *Germany v B and Germany v D and others* ECR [2010 I-10979], on exclusion clauses (Article 12 of the Qualification Directive).

[136] See Article 31(6) Recast, which permits that an examination procedure, in accordance with the basic principles and guarantees of Chapter II, be accelerated and/or conducted at the border in accordance with Article 43 Recast in seven exhaustive cases.

[137] See Article 14(2) Recast.

[138] See Article 31 (7) Recast.

[139] See Article 46 (4) Recast.

[140] See Article 46 (6) Recast.

[141] See UNHCR (2012), see footnote 116, p. 26.

reasons of public security or public order under national law.' As such, Article 31(6)(g) Recast reintroduces Article 23(4)(m) of the original Asylum Procedures Directive. Given that what constitutes "danger" as well as "national security" and "public order" are subject to a wide margin of appreciation the inclusion of such a ground for accelerated procedures is questionable.[142]

With regard to the "Safe Third Country" (STC),[143] "Safe Country of Origin" (SCO)[144] and "First Country of Asylum" (FCA), the compromise text of the Directive retains these concepts with some changes rather than removing them completely, despite their alleged violation of international refugee law.[145] Asylum-seekers may see their application rejected in the admissibility procedure on the grounds of the above concepts, the meaning of which is rather ambiguous. Member States may justify the inadmissibility of asylum applications made by individuals who, before arriving, have passed through countries considered safe especially if made at the border. The 1951 Geneva Convention, and in particular, the *non-refoulement* clause in Article 33, does not forbid them from doing so. Specifically, Member States may reject an application when asylum-seekers are deemed protected—either in fact or by law- or could have obtained protection in those countries.

The first difficulty encountered with these concepts is determining whether a country is "safe" particularly with regard to SCO. The Directive no longer includes a common list of STCs, which was included in an Annex by the Council[146] and Article 36 Recast explicitly refers to the need to conduct an individual examination of the application and that the asylum-seeker has not submitted 'any serious grounds for considering the country not to be a safe country of origin in his/her particular circumstances and in terms of his/her qualification as a refugee or a person eligible for subsidiary protection in accordance with the Qualification Directive.' In addition, Recital 30 provides that a key consideration for the well-foundedness of an application for international protection is the safety of the applicant in his/her country of origin. A third country can be regarded as a SCO by a Member State for a particular applicant unless he/she presents counter-

---

142 Idem.

143 See Articles 38 (STC) and 39 (European STC) of the revised Directive.

144 The generic formulation of Article 30(5) of the original Asylum Procedures Directive and of Article 37 (3) of the new Directive permits wide divergences in the information sources used by Member States to determine SCOs. This fact, combined with major differences in the designation criteria applied, inevitably results in inconsistency in the designation of SCO; see UNHCR (2010), see footnote 150 in Chap. 2, which includes a comparative study of three Member States with a public national list of safe country of origin. At the time of UNHCR's research, France had designated 15 countries as safe, Germany 29 and the United Kingdom 24. Little correlation was found between the lists and only one country (Ghana) appeared on the list of all three States—and for the United Kingdom, Ghana was considered a SCO for male applicants only; see also Costello (2005), see footnote 78 in Chap. 2, at 66–67.

145 For critical commentary, Refs. [61, 62]; S. Da Lomba (2004), see footnote 20; Refs. [63–67]; Ippolito and Velluti (2011), see footnote 55 in Chap. 2, at 54–56; Refs. [68, 69].

146 See old Article 29 of the original Directive, now repealed.

indications. Hence the latter no longer need to be "serious." In a similar vein, Recital 33 refers to "valid," and no longer "serious," reasons to consider the country not to be safe in his/her particular circumstances, the designation of the country as safe can no longer be considered relevant for him/her. Moreover, Article 16 Recast concerning the content of the personal interview does seem to provide the possibility for the applicant to use any such necessary counter-indications given that it states that 'the applicant is given an adequate opportunity to present elements needed to substantiate the application in accordance with Article 4 of the Qualification Directive' concerning assessment of facts and circumstances.

However, the Recast Directive still includes national designation of third countries as SCO.[147] Some significant changes have been introduced to take into account the fact that the complexity of the decision as to whether a third country is a SCO may lead to errors and also that the politicized decision-making process may often lead to foreign policy concerns influencing the objectivity of the assessment.[148] Article 37(2) Recast envisages a regular review of the situation in third countries designated as safe in consideration of the fact that human rights situations change rapidly and thus lists of SCO should be subject to constant and regular review.[149] Article 37(3) Recast provides that 'the assessment of whether a country is a safe country of origin in accordance with this Article shall be based on a range of sources of information, including in particular information from other Member States, the European Asylum Support Office, the UNHCR, the Council of Europe and other relevant international organizations.' With regard to FCA, the new formulation in Article 35 Recast provides the applicant with the possibility to rebut the presumption of safety in cases where the FCA concept is applied. However, the entire burden of rebutting this presumption rests on the applicant. As to the notion of the European STC, Article 39 Recast requires Member States periodically to inform the Commission about the countries to which the European STC is applied. However, UNHCR rightly continues to question the utility and consistency with international refugee law of the European STC concept also in consideration of the fact that no minimum principles and guarantees underlie the procedure under Article 39 Recast.

On the basis of these concepts, access to territory and to an asylum procedure may be denied altogether to asylum-seekers who may have protection needs.

---

[147] See Articles 36(2) and 37 of the revised Directive.

[148] See Costello (2005), see footnote 78 in Chap. 2, at 66.

[149] See e.g. *NA. v. The United Kingdom,* Appl. No. 25904/07, paras 112 and 119, where the ECtHR stated that 'A full and *ex nunc* assessment is called for as the situation in a country of destination may change in the course of time. Even though the historical position is of interest in so far as it may shed light on the current situation and its likely evolution, it is the present conditions which are decisive and it is therefore necessary to take into account information that has come to light after the final decision taken by the domestic authorities;' see also Article 46(3) Recast which provides that 'Member States shall ensure that an effective remedy provides for a full and *ex nunc* examination of both facts and points of law.'

Such a denial could be at variance with international refugee law. Costello cogently predicted back in 2005 that:

> the FCA, STC and SCO provisions will undermine both access to and the integrity of asylum procedures in the enlarged EU. They will increase the likelihood of error in asylum determinations and inevitably lead to *refoulement* as refugees are deported or refused access to proper procedures. As such, the Directives embodies *lowest common denominator law-making at its worst*,[150] as the varied exclusionary procedural practices of the Member States have come to be incorporated for the first time in a legally binding instrument.[151]

The legitimacy of these decisions is questionable considering the strong differences that exist in the standard of protection between the EU and third countries, both of origin and transit. Moreover, there is no uniform guarantee for asylum-seekers in relation to admissibility, accelerated and border procedures and thus no certainty that the STC concept will be applied to them according to the same standard of safety across the EU.[152] Morgades argues that returning asylum-seekers who apply for asylum in a Member State but who have not arrived there directly from the country where persecution is feared creates the "externalization of the asylum function," on the basis of which the responsibility for asylum for people who have not arrived directly in a Member State is transferred to other countries where asylum-seekers have not applied for protection.[153] Problems of compliance with international human rights standards as well as Article 18 of the EU Charter therefore remain.[154]

From the foregoing analysis, it may be argued that in spite of the changes introduced by the Recast Directive, there is still an overwhelming concern for preserving Member States' prerogatives and powers with a focus on efficiency rather than the strengthening of asylum-seekers procedural safeguards.[155]

3.4 The Revised Reception Conditions Directive: Towards More Harmonized and Dignified Standards of Living?

Fair and efficient reception conditions for asylum-seekers during the examination of their application for international protection constitute an essential part of any asylum system[156] in that they guarantee that applicants are prepared for both

[150] Emphasis added.

[151] See Costello (2005), see footnote 78 in Chap. 2, at 36–37.

[152] See UNHCR (2010), see footnote 150 in Chap. 2.

[153] See Ref. [70]; on the issue of extraterritorial processing, see e.g. S. Kneebone, C. McDowell and G. Morrell (2006), see footnote 18, at 507–508; Ref. [71–74].

[154] See Ippolito and Velluti (2011), see footnote 55 in Chap. 2, at 54–56.

[155] See Ref. [75], at 25–38.

[156] See Ref. [76], at p. 3.

possible outcomes of the asylum procedure, either integration into the host society upon recognition or sustainable and dignified return after a full examination of their claim concludes that they are not in need of international protection.[157] At the same time adequate reception conditions are a conduit for a fair and efficient asylum procedure.[158]

The process of recasting the Reception Conditions Directive was troublesome and difficult as the one for the Asylum Procedures Directive and the agreed text of the Council and the European Parliament presents similar gaps and inconsistencies. In December 2008, the European Commission presented a recast proposal for the Reception Conditions Directive,[159] aimed at harmonizing divergent national practices, in order to ensure that asylum-seekers would enjoy an equivalent standard of reception conditions in all Member States.[160] The European Parliament adopted its position on that proposal in May 2009.[161] However, in June 2011 after no final agreement was reached on the text in the Council of Ministers, the European Commission published an amended recast proposal of the Reception Conditions Directive.[162] In June 2013, as part of the EU asylum package for the second phase of CEAS,[163] the European Parliament endorsed the political agreement of the Council of Ministers.[164]

Critically, the amended Commission Recast Reception Conditions Directive proposal (on which the agreed text of the Council and the European Parliament is largely based) reduces the safeguards for asylum-seekers with regard to adequate reception conditions in a number of key provisions compared to the 2008 Commission Recast proposal. Additionally, it increases the possibility for Member States to derogate from the guarantees it is supposed to set. Arguably, the initial aim to ensure higher standards of reception conditions by way of harmonization has been seriously watered down.

Among the positive changes introduced, there is the extension of the personal scope of the Directive to applicants for subsidiary protection[165] and clarification of

---

157 Idem.

158 Idem.

159 See Refs. [77–79]. The Proposal drew on several soft law measures adopted by the UNHCR and the Council of Europe Committee of Ministers on measures of detention of asylum-seekers. See e.g. Refs. [80, 81]; and Ref. [82].

160 Denmark, Ireland and the United Kingdom will not be bound by the new Directive, but the UK will continue to apply the 2003 rules.

161 See Ref. [83].

162 See Ref. [84].

163 For press releases and news reports on the EU asylum package, see European Commission (2013) and ECRE (2013), see footnote 113.

164 The text of the political agreement endorsed by the European Parliament in plenary session in June 2013 is available at: http://register.consilium.europa.eu/pdf/en/12/st14/st14112-re01.en12.pdf.

165 See Article 2(a) Recast.

its geographical scope by explicitly including transit zones in its scope[166]; the extension of the definition of family members[167]; minor and dependent adult applicants will enjoy more guarantees to be housed jointly with family members and relatives[168]; the obligation for Member States to ensure access to the labour market no later than 9 months after the application for international protection is lodged as this will help asylum-seekers to be more integrated in the society of the host country and make them more self-sufficient[169]; the limitation of circumstances in which reception conditions can be entirely withdrawn as this will reduce the circumstances in which asylum-seekers may become destitute[170]; as to health care, the Recast Directive explicitly includes essential treatment of serious mental disorders and, where needed, appropriate mental health care[171]; the strengthening of safeguards for vulnerable groups[172]; and Member States must ensure that persons who have been subject to torture, rape or other serious acts of violence receive the necessary treatment, in particular access to appropriate medical and psychological treatment or care. Furthermore, those working with such persons must have had, and must continue to receive, the appropriate training and be bound by confidentiality rules.[173] However, in spite of these improved reception conditions the Recast Directive also seems to be lowering down certain standards. For instance, with regard to family members Article 2(c) Recast requires the family ties to have been established already in the country of origin. This fails to accommodate family ties that may have been formed while residing in a third country during flight and may prevent refugees from enjoying the right to family unity contrary to the Geneva Convention.[174]

---

[166] See Article 3(1) Recast.

[167] See Article 2 (c) Recast.

[168] See Recital 18(a), Articles 12, 18(2)(a)(c) Recast.

[169] See Article 15 (1) Recast.

[170] See Article 20 Recast.

[171] See Article 19 Recast.

[172] See Articles 21–25 Recast.

[173] See Article 25 Recast.

[174] The Refugee Convention provides protection for the refugee family in various articles without explicitly mentioning family unity or reunification, e.g. Article 4 refers to refugees' 'freedom as regards the religious education of their children'; Article 12(2) provides that '[…] rights attaching to marriage, shall be respected […]'; Article 22 concerns the public education of children in elementary school and beyond; para 2 of the annexed schedule, concerning travel documents, notes that children may be included in the travel document of a parent or, in exceptional circumstances, of another adult refugee. Refugees' "essential right" to family unity was the subject of recommendations approved unanimously by the Conference of Plenipotentiaries that adopted the final text of the Convention, UN Conference of Plenipotentiaries on the Status of Refugees and Stateless Persons, *Final Act of the United Nations Conference of Plenipotentiaries on the Status of Refugees and Stateless Persons*, 25 July 1951, A/CONF.2/108/Rev.1, available at: http://www.refworld.org/docid/40a8a7394.html. Recommendation B; for further analysis of family unification and refugees, see Ref. [85].

As to material reception conditions, Article 17(5) Recast proposes a system according to which the amount of material reception conditions must be determined on the basis of points of reference established by each Member State in law or in practice to ensure adequate standards of living for nationals. The minimum level of social welfare assistance is mentioned by way of example of such point of reference. However, Article 17(5) Recast also allows Member States to 'grant less favourable treatment to asylum applicants compared to nationals in this respect, where it is duly justified.' This may potentially lead to Member States granting unacceptably low levels of material reception conditions as the extent to which treatment may be less favourable compared to nationals is not qualified and could well be below what is an adequate standard of living as required under Article 17(1) Recast. With regard to the possibility of Member States' withdrawing material reception conditions, although Article 20(1) Recast identifies clear grounds for enabling Member States to withdraw them it still leaves them with a wide margin of discretion. The withdrawal or reduction of reception conditions below an adequate standard of living is not consistent with the requirements of human rights law. The possibility for Member States to completely withdraw reception conditions should only be allowed where it is shown that the asylum-seeker concerned has sufficient means of support ensuring an adequate standard of living.[175]

The most controversial aspect of the Reception Conditions Directive is the detention of asylum-seekers[176] and consequently many of the changes introduced aim at improving various aspects of the detention rules which are considered to be at variance with international refugee and human rights law.[177] The detention of asylum-seekers for immigration control purposes—apart from the most exceptional circumstances as prescribed by international law and standards- is inherently undesirable. It places undue hardship on asylum-seekers and in the great majority of cases can be replaced by less repressive alternatives.[178] Moreover, the use of detention is not conducive to good integration in the country of asylum as the first experience of the asylum-seeker is one of deprivation of liberty, which can often be prolonged; it also delays the start of such integration.[179] Non-custodial alternatives to detention are very effective in achieving the legitimate purposes for which they can be used, while being less restrictive to asylum-seekers' rights.[180]

[175] See *MSS v. Belgium and Greece*, Application No. 30696/09, Judgment of 21 January 2011, para 263, where the ECtHR held that the fact that an asylum-seeker had spent months in living in a state of extreme poverty, unable to cater for his most basic needs in combination with prolonged uncertainty and the total lack of any prospects of his situation improving amounted to a violation of Article 3 ECHR.

[176] The relevant provisions are clearly modeled on the corresponding provisions on detention of irregularly staying third country nationals for the purpose of removal in the Returns Directive, see Articles 15, 16 and 17 of Directive 2008/115/EC.

[177] For critical commentary on the issue of detention, see Refs. [86–88].

[178] See Ref. [89].

[179] Idem.

[180] Idem.

Nevertheless, immigration detention is increasingly routine, even automatic across Europe, with asylum-seekers being an easy target for detention.[181] Often detention is justified on the basis that categories of immigrants, including asylum-seekers, are "illegal" either entering a state's territory without authorization or in staying after they have been told to leave.[182] While International human rights law limits detention, the level of protection afforded to migrants is often weaker than in other contexts as states' migration control powers remain intact in this area, reflecting an uneasy tension between the universal right to liberty and states' border control prerogatives.[183]

Starting with the positive changes, Recital 15 Recast provides that detention of asylum-seekers should be applied in line with the underlying principle that a person should not be held in detention for the sole reason that he/she is seeking international protection, in accordance with Member States' international legal obligations and in particular Article 31 of the Geneva Convention.[184] It also states that detention should be subject to the principle of necessity and proportionality with regard to the manner and to the purpose of such detention. Where an asylum-seeker is held in detention he/she should be able to have effective access to the necessary procedural guarantees such as judicial remedy before a national court. Moreover, Recital 16 Recast states that applicants who are in detention should be treated with full respect of human dignity and their reception should be specifically designed to meet their needs in that situation. In particular, Member States should ensure that Article 37 of the 1989 UN Convention on the Rights of the Child is applied. Recital 17(a) provides that detention of asylum-seekers should be a measure of last resort and may be applied only after all non-custodial alternative measures to detention have been duly examined in order to better ensure the asylum-seeker's physical and psychological integrity.

Any alternative measure to detention must respect the fundamental human rights of asylum-seekers. This is reinforced by Article 8(2) Recast which provides that the use of detention has to be based on an individual assessment and only if other less coercive alternative measures cannot be applied effectively. Moreover, an applicant for international protection can only be detained if at least one of the grounds listed in Article 8(3) Recast applies. However, Recital 15(b) Recast does not exclude the application of other grounds such as detention grounds in the framework of criminal proceedings, applicable in the national legal order unrelated to the TCN's or stateless person's application for international protection. The new rules on detention also provide important guarantees for detained applicants. Article 9(1) Recast provides that detention shall be for as short a period as possible

[181] See Costello (2012), see footnote 177.

[182] Ibidem, at pp. 258–259.

[183] Idem.

[184] See also new Article 8(1) Recast. Goodwin-Gill notes that 'comparatively few states have taken any formal steps to incorporate the exemption from penalties required by Article 31 [of the Geneva Convention] [...]. Even where legislative provisions exist, however, refugees and asylum-seekers can still face loss of liberty,' see Ref. [90], at p. 226.

and shall only be maintained for as long as the grounds set out in Article 8(3) Recast are applicable. Asylum-seekers will be informed in writing about the reasons for their detention and the ways to challenge it[185] and will also be able to request free legal assistance and representation, in a language they understand or are reasonably supposed to understand.[186] Furthermore, detained asylum-seekers must have prompt access to rapid judicial review[187] and as a rule applicants for international protection must be detained in special reception facilities.[188] If this is not possible prison accommodation is allowed, but only under the condition that the applicant is kept separate from criminals. Finally, a regime providing additional safeguards has been established in relation to the detention of vulnerable persons and persons with special reception needs.[189] Noteworthy is the removal of any reference to the ill-defined notion of "continued detention" in Article 11 Recast. The Recast Directive specifies that unaccompanied minors shall only be detained as a measure of last resort and after having established that other less coercive alternative measures cannot be applied effectively. It shall be for the shortest period of time and all efforts shall be made to release the detained minors and place them in accommodation suitable for minors. Moreover, a best interest assessment has been envisaged in case Member States make use of the possibility to place an unaccompanied child aged 16 or more in an accommodation centre for adults as foreseen by Article 24(2), subpara 2 Recast.

However, despite the inclusion of new provisions aimed at strengthening the procedural guarantees in relation to detention the new Directive still presents some significant shortcomings. AI points out that under the Recast Directive there is still a risk of condoning extensive use of detention of asylum-seekers. In particular, under Article 8 Recast, which sets out the grounds for detention, an asylum-seeker may be detained in order to 'determine or verify his identity or nationality.' This provision, as worded, goes beyond what is allowed under the UNHCR guidelines on detention of asylum-seekers,[190] which mention the verification of identity only in cases where identity may be undetermined or in dispute. Article 8(3)(a) Recast should have stated explicitly that detention on this ground should only be possible if he or she clearly refuses to cooperate in order to frustrate the process of identification. With no such reference there is a real risk that it will encourage systematic detention of asylum-seekers in practice based on the assumption that detention is in any case necessary in order to allow verification of an asylum-

[185] See Article 9(3) Recast, which provides that detention shall be ordered in writing and that the detention order shall state the reasons in fact and in law on which it is based. This provision is in line with the jurisprudence of the ECtHR, see e.g. *Lokpo and Touré v. Hungary*, Application No. 10816/10, Judgment of 20 September 2011, para 24.

[186] See Article 9(2) subpara 2 and (5) and (6) Recast and also Article 10(5) Recast.

[187] See Article 9(2) Recast.

[188] See Article 10(1) Recast.

[189] See Article 11 Recast.

[190] See Ref. [91]; see also Ref. [92], which replace the 1999 Guidelines.

seeker's identity or nationality.[191] ECRE criticizes the fact that asylum-seekers can be kept in prisons if no specialized detention facilities are available, even though they would be kept separate from ordinary prisoners.[192] The lack of precise time limits for the detention of asylum-seekers is also questionable. Member States' discretion on imposing restrictions on the legal aid granted to asylum-seekers[193] is also another limitation of the new Reception Conditions Directive. Article 9(3) Recast envisages the possibility that the detention order can be in a language that the asylum-seeker is 'reasonably supposed to understand.' Such a standard is not in line with Article 5(2) ECHR according to which 'everyone who is arrested shall be informed promptly, in a language which he understands, of the reasons for his arrest and of any charge against him.'[194] Another disconcerting limitation of the Recast Directive is that detention in prison accommodation is allowed under Article 10(6)(a) Recast, where Member States are obliged to resort to such accommodation in cases where specialized detention facilities are temporarily not available. As the European Committee for the Prevention of Torture (CPT) rightly observes, 'even if the actual conditions of detention for these persons in the establishments concerned are adequate -which has not always been the case—the CPT considers such an approach to be fundamentally flawed. A prison is by definition not a suitable place in which to detain someone who is neither convicted nor suspected of a criminal offence.'[195] Moreover, while minor asylum-seekers can only be detained as a last resort and unaccompanied minors cannot be kept in prison or together with adults, detention is still permitted, albeit only in exceptional circumstances.[196] Hence, it may be argued that in spite of its purported aims the Directive itself presents 'the same attachment to detention as a means of policing the EU border that traditional states have maintained'[197] with a persistence of territoriality even in the context of a discourse that aspires to surpass it.[198]

The foregoing analysis shows that overall the Recast Reception Conditions Directive does not provide a coherent set of adequate material reception conditions and procedural guarantees for asylum-seekers, particularly those who are vulnerable and in need of higher levels of protection. Various contradictions and tensions beset the Recast Directive impeding it to fully ensure a dignifying standard of living for asylum-seekers.

[191] See ECRE (2011), see footnote 156, at p. 8.

[192] See Article 10 Recast; ECRE (2011), see footnote 156, at p. 13.

[193] See new Article 9(6) and (7); see further ECRE (2011), see footnote 156, at p. 12.

[194] See *Conka v. Belgium*, Application No. 51564/99, Judgment of 5 February 2002, para 50.

[195] See Ref. [93]

[196] See further, ECRE (2011), see footnote 156, at pp. 16–18; on the issue of asylum-seeking children's detention, see Ref. [94].

[197] See Ref. [95], at p. 145.

[198] See Ref. [96], at pp. 221–222.

3.5 Challenges to Harmonization: The Absence of a True Dialectic Between a Rights-Based Approach and a Migration Control-Based Approach

The reform of key legislative instruments of CEAS overall has not led to significant changes from an asylum-seekers' human rights perspective. Clearly, the challenges posed by the goal of harmonization have been too great for the EU legislature to overcome, despite attempts to do so, as exemplified by the various recast processes. Progress in amending the legislation has been stifled by lengthy and difficult negotiations, the extensive use of measures of flexibility and heterogeneous interpretation and implementation of adopted "common" measures. The untouched optional derogations and scope for discretionary measures effectively undermine the pursuit of harmonization.

The root-causes of this *status quo* are not to be sought in a deliberate unwillingness to act[199] but rather in the primacy and strong influence of classical conceptions of state sovereignty and related principles of territorial supremacy and self-preservation, which impact particularly on asylum decision-making.[200] Undeniably, there is a strong relationship between refugee status determination, the granting of asylum and state sovereignty. This necessary "bond" stems from the effects and consequences that follow from decisions made in the procedure: the inclusion of a new member in a (nation-)state's society, and the very nature and purpose of the institution of asylum as a means of correcting a state's failure to protect its "own" citizens.[201] Hence, sovereignty is not merely a legitimacy token for state action but becomes a state's claim to determine and protect what constitutes the boundary between the "inside" and the "outside" and establishes the linkage between political authority and clearly demarcated territories and borders.[202]

At the same time, we have seen that not all is lost for those advocating a more human rights-based approach and that there is scope for optimism. Far from being some form of dystopian society, the creation and further development of CEAS is in effect slowly but steadily entrenching a human rights discourse at all levels and in all spheres of policy-making: Member States clearly have to "defend" their measures, actions and decisions against a set of fundamental rights' "benchmarks" enshrined in International refugee law and European human rights law. More specifically, developments concerning CEAS illustrate the significant problems posed by the adherence to classical conceptions of sovereignty and its related paradigms and values.

---

199 It should be re-called that asylum procedures pertain to state administrative justice and, consequently, they are judicial procedures that are imbued with strong national cultural and traditional procedural connotations, see Refs. [97, 98].

200 On the issue of state sovereignty, see above, infra Chap. 1.

201 See Refs. [99, 100].

202 See Refs. [101, 102].

A more apposite approach, therefore, is one which relies on a "floating" conception of sovereignty,[203] which takes into account how states are exposed to mutating global, regional and local processes and how the manner in which European governance operates in respect of the individual is also necessarily changing. In this way we acknowledge the need to embrace a more open, reflexive and cooperative conception of sovereignty.

It would be naïve if not utopian to maintain that change, as suggested above, should be introduced through the legislative route. An alternative avenue instead, which is more grounded in reality, is to propose that the pursuit of such objective be achieved via the judiciary. Legal norms can be subject, by their very nature, to multiple interpretations because of their required connotations of universality and generality. Historically, it has often been up to courts to shape and refine the actual content of legal rules, and in relation to European law, to the European Courts. As evidenced by many landmark rulings, their jurisprudence has had a truly transformative impact on national legal systems,[204] whether directly or indirectly and whether at the will or against countries' assent. It is therefore to them that the present investigation now turns to.

References

1. Council of the European Union (2013a) Recast of the Dublin regulation: enhancing the efficiency of the functioning of the current system. Luxembourg, 7 June 2013, 10526/1/13 REV 1. Available via http://www.consilium.europa.eu/uedocs/cms_data/docs/pressdata/en/jha/137418.pdf
2. Council of the European Union (2013b) Position of the council at first reading with a view to the adoption of a regulation of the european parliament and of the council establishing the criteria and mechanisms for determining the member state responsible for examining an application for international protection lodged in one of the member states by a third-country national or a stateless person (recast), 15605/2/12 REV 2, Brussels 31 May 2013. Available via http://register.consilium.europa.eu/pdf/en/12/st15/st15605-re02.en12.pdf
3. European Commission (2013) EU puts common European asylum system in place News, Available via http://ec.europa.eu/commission_2010-2014/malmstrom/news/archives/2013/06/20130612_en.htm
4. European Parliament (2013) LIBE adopted the asylum package and Schengen evaluation mechanism, News, Committee on Civil Liberties, Justice and Home Affairs, 10.06.2013. Available via http://www.europarl.europa.eu/committees/en/libe/home.html
5. Filzwieser C, Liebminger B (2009) Dublin II-Verordnung. Bwv-Berliner Wissenschafts-verlag, Berlin

[203] See above, Chap. 2, Sect. 2.1.

[204] The study of the impact of the case law of the European Courts on national legal systems is beyond the scope of the present investigation and the reader is directed to selected literature on the subject. On the ECJ, see e.g. Refs. [103–105]; on the ECtHR, see e.g. Refs. [106–108]. For more general academic commentary on the interaction between the international and national legal regimes, see Refs. [109, 110].

6. Frelick B (2008) Stuck in a revolving door. iraqis and other asylum-seekers and migrants at the Greece/Turkey entrance to the European union november 2008, Human Rights Watch. Available via http://www.hrw.org/sites/default/files/reports/greeceturkey1108webwcover.pdf
7. Maiani F, Vevstad V (2010) Chapter 1: distribution of applicants for international protection and protected persons' in european parliament, directorate-general for internal policies, policy department C, citizens' rights and constitutional affairs, 'setting up a common european asylum system. Report on the application of existing instruments and proposals for the new system,' PE 425.622, Brussels 2010
8. Nash C, Kok S (2005) The way forward: towards fair and efficient asylum systems in Europe,' brussels, ECRE, 13 Sept 2005. Available via http://www.ecre.org/resources/policy_papers/219
9. UNHCR (2002) Observations on the European Commission's Proposal for a Council Regulation Establishing the Criteria and Mechanisms for Determining the Member State Responsible for Examining an Asylum Application Lodged in one of the Member States by a Third-Country National (COM(2001) 447 final). UNHCR, Geneva 2002
10. UNHCR (2006) The Dublin II regulation: a UNHCR discussion paper. UNHCR, Geneva, Available via http://www.unhcr.org/refworld/docid/4445fe344.html
11. UNHCR (2008) Comments on the European Commission's Proposal for a recast of the Regulation of the European Parliament and of the Council establishing the criteria and mechanisms for determining the Member State responsible for examining an application for international protection lodged in one of the Member States by a third country national or a stateless person (Dublin II) (Com(2008) 820, 3 December 2008) and the European Commission's Proposal for a recast of the Regulation of the European Parliament and of the Council concerning the establishment of 'Eurodac' for a comparison of fingerprints for the effective application of [the Dublin 1 1] Regulation] (COM(2008) 825, 3 December 2008)', 1–2 March 2009. Available Via http://www.unhcr.org/cgi-bin/texis/vtx/search?pagesearch&query=COM%/282008%29+825%2C++December+2008&x=0&y=0
12. ECRE (2006) Report on the application of the Dublin II regulation in Europe', 169 (March 2006). Available at http://www.ecre.org/component/content/article/57-policy-papers/135-report-on-the-application-of-the-dublin-ii-regulation-in-europe.html
13. Garlick M (2006) The EU discussions on extraterritorial processing: solution or conundrum?' Int J Refugee Law 18(3/4):601–629
14. Gilbert G (2004) Is Europe living up to its obligations to refugees?' Eur J Int Law 15(5):963–987
15. Guild E (2004) Seeking Asylum: storm clouds between international commitments and EU legislative measures. Eur Law Rev 29(2):198–218
16. Battjes H (2011) Mutual trust in asylum matters: the Dublin system. In: Meijers Committee, (Standing Committee of Experts on International Immigration, Refugee and Criminal Law) The Principle of Mutual Trust in European Asylum, Migration and Criminal Law. FORUM, Institute for Multicultural Affairs), Utrecht, pp 8–18
17. Maiani F, Hruschka C (2011) Le partage des responsabilités dans l'espace Dublin, entre confiance mutuelle—et sécurité des demandeurs d'asile. Asyl 2:12–19
18. Brandl U (2003) Distribution of Asylum-seekers in Europe? Dublin II regulation determining the responsibility for examining an asylum application. In: Dias Urbano de Souza C, De Bruycker P (eds) The emergence of a European asylum policy. Bruylant, Brussels, pp 33–69
19. European Commission (2005) Staff working paper on revisiting the dublin convention: developing community legislation for determining which Member State is responsible for considering an application for asylum submitted in one of the Member States, SEC(2000) 522
20. Kneebone S, McDowell C, Morrell G (2006) A Mediterranean solution? Chances of success. Int J Refugee Law 18(3/4):492–508
21. Da Lomba S (2004) The right to seek refugee status in the European Union. Intersentia), New York

22. European Parliament (2008) Report on the evaluation of the Dublin system. Committee on Civil Liberties, Justice and Home Affairs 2 July 2008, A6-0287/2008, 12)
23. Papadimitriou PN, Papageorgiou IF (2005) The New "Dubliners": implementation of European council regulation 343/2003 (Dublin-II) by the Greek authorities. J Refugee Stud 18(3):299–318
24. UNHCR (2007) The return to Greece of asylum-seekers with "Interrupted" claims,' Geneva, UNHCR, July 2007. Available via http://www.unhcr.org/refworld/pdfid/46b889b32.pdf
25. Amnesty International (2010) The Dublin II Trap' (March 2010). Available via http://www.amnesty.org/en/library/info/EUR25/001/2010/en, pp 35–41
26. ECRE (2008) Sharing responsibility for refugee protection in Europe: Dublin reconsidered,' 15 (March 2008). Available via http://www.ecre.org/component/content/article/57-policy-papers/134-sharing-responsibility-for-refugee-protection-in-europe-dublin-reconsidered.html
27. ECRE (2009) Comments on the European council on refugees and exiles on the European commission proposal to recast the Dublin regulation, Brussels, ECRE, April 2009. Available via http://www.ecre.org/files/ECRE_Response_to_Recast_Dublin_Regulation_2009.pdf
28. European Commission (2007) Green paper on the future common European asylum system, COM(2007) 301 final, 6 June. 2007
29. European Parliament (2008) Evaluation of the Dublin system (Own Initiative Report), INI(2008) 2262, 2 July 2008, para 2
30. European Parliament (2010) Position adopted at first reading on 7 May 2009 with a view to the adoption of Regulation (EC) No…/2009 of the European Parliament and of the Council establishing the criteria and mechanisms for determining the Member State responsible for examining an application for international protection lodged in one of the Member States by a third-country national or a stateless person (recast), OJ C 5 August 2010, No. 212, E/371
31. Council of Ministers (2010) Discussion Paper No. 15561/10, 29 October 2010
32. Council of Ministers (2011) Discussion Paper No. 16782/11, 14 November 2011
33. UNHCR (2013) Statement on the reception conditions of asylum-seekers under the Dublin procedure, Issued in the context of a reference for a preliminary ruling addressed to Court of Justice of the European Union by the French Council of State lodged on 18 April 2011—CIMADE and GISTI v. Ministry of the Interior (Case C-179/11), 1 August 2011. Available via http://www.refworld.org/docid/4e37b5902.html
34. Eaton J (2012) The internal protection alternative under European union law: examining the recast qualification directive. Int J Refugee Law 24(4):765–792
35. Kosar D (2013) Inclusion before Exclusion or vice versa: what the qualification directive and the court of justice do (Not) say. Int J Refugee Law 25(1):87–119
36. Gil-Bazo MT (2006) Refugee status, subsidiary protection, and the right to be granted Asylum under EC law, new issues in refugee research. Research Paper No. 136, Geneva, UNHCR, November 2006
37. Da Lomba S (2011) The EU qualification directive and refugee Sur Place. In: Goudappel F, Raulus HS (eds) The future of asylum in the European union. Problems, proposals and human rights. Springer, The Hague, pp 43–64
38. Lambert H (2006) The EU asylum qualification directive, its impact on the jurisprudence of the United Kingdom and international law. Int Comp Law Q 55(1):161–192
39. Noll G (2006) Evidentiary assessment in refugee status determination and the EU qualification directive. Eur Public Law 12(1):295–317
40. Peers S (2005) Human rights, asylum and European community law. Refugee Survey Q 24(2):24–38
41. European Commission (2010) Report from the commission to the European parliament and the council on the application of directive 2004/83/EC of 29 April 2004 on minimum standards for the qualification and status of third country nationals or stateless persons as refugees or as persons who otherwise need international protection and the content of the

protection, COM(2010) 314 final, 16 Jun. 2010; ECRE/European Legal Network on Asylum (ELENA), The Impact of the EU Qualification Directive on International Protection, ("ELENA Survey"), Brussels, ECRE, Oct. 2008. Available via http://www.ecre.org/files/ECRE_QD_study_full.pdf
42. UNHCR (2007) Asylum in the European Union. A study of the implementation of the qualification directive. UNHCR, Geneva, Available via http://www.unhcr.org/refworld/docid/473050632.html
43. UNHCR (2005) Refugee status determination, identifying who is a refugee. Available via http://www.unhcr.org/refworld/pdfid/462f6d982.pdf, p. 44
44. Musalo K, Moore J, Boswell RA (2007) Refugee law and policy. a comparative and international approach. Carolina Academic Press, Durham
45. Musalo K (2002) Claims for protection based on religion or belief: analysis and proposed conclusions, legal and protection policy research series. UNHCR, Department of International Protection, Geneva
46. Teitgen-Colly C (2006) The European Union and asylum: an illusion of protection. Comm Mark Law Rev 43(6):1503–1566
47. European Parliament and Council of the European Union (2011) Directive 2011/95/EU of the European Parliament and of the Council of 13 December 2011 on standards for the qualification of third-country nationals or stateless persons as beneficiaries of international protection, for a uniform status for refugees or for persons eligible for subsidiary protection, and for the content of the protection granted (recast), OJ L 337/9, 20.12.2011
48. GHK (2006) Impact assessment studies on the future development of measures on the qualification and status of third country nationals or stateless persons as persons in need of international protection and on the content of the protection granted, based on Council Directive 2004/83/EC and The future development of measures on procedures in MS for granting and withdrawing refugee status, based on Council Directive 2005/85/EC, Multiple framework service contract JLS/2006/A1/004
49. Hathaway J Foster M (2003) Internal protection/relocation/flight alternative. In: Feller E et al (eds) Refugee protection in international law: UNHCR's global consultations on international protection. CUP, Cambridge, pp 357–417
50. UNHCR (1999) IPA position paper: relocating internally as a reasonable alternative to seeking asylum (the So-Called "Internal Flight Alternative" or "Relocation Principle", February 1999. Available via http://www.refworld.org/docid/3ae6b336c.html
51. Spijkerboer T, Arbaoui Y (2010) Council directive 2005/85/EC of 1 December 2005 on minimum standards on procedures in Member States for granting and withdrawing refugee status. In: Hailbronner K (ed) EU Immigration and asylum law—commentary. Hart, Oxford, pp 1227–1350
52. European Commission (2011) Amended proposal for a directive of the European parliament and of the council on common procedures for granting and withdrawing international protection status (Recast) COM (2011) 319 final
53. European Commission (2009) Proposal for a directive of the European parliament and of the council on minimum standards on procedures in member states for granting and withdrawing international protection (COM (2009)554, 21 October 2009)
54. European Parliament (2013) Civil liberties committee backs plan to improve asylum procedures. Press release. Available via http://www.europarl.europa.eu/news/en/pressroom/content/20130422IPR07521/html/Civil-Liberties-Committee-backs-plan-to-improve-asylum-procedures
55. European Commission (2013) News: the EP votes on the common European asylum system. Available via http://ec.europa.eu/dgs/home-affairs/what-is-new/news/news/2013/20130612_01_en.htm
56. Council of the European Union (2013) Amended proposal for a directive of the European Parliament and of the Council on Common Procedures for Granting and Withdrawing International Protection Status (Recast) [First Reading]—Analysis of final compromise text with a view to agreement, Interinstitutional File: 2009/0165 (COD); ECRE (2013), 'JHA

Council adopts recast Asylum Procedures and Reception Conditions Directives and the Dublin Regulation. Available via http://ecre.org/component/content/article/70-weekly-bulletin-articles/374-jha-council-adopts-recast-asylum-procedures-and-reception-conditions-directives-and-the-dublin-regulation.html
57. UNHCR (2012) UNHCR Comments on the European commission's Amended proposal for a directive of the european parliament and of the council on common procedures for granting and withdrawing international protection status (Recast) COM (2011) 319 final. Available via http://www.unhcr.org/4f35256c9.pdf
58. European Parliament (2011) Texts Adopted at the sitting of Wednesday 6 Aril 2011, P7_TA-Prov(2011)0136, Amendment 13. Available via http://www.europarl.europa.eu/sides/getDoc.do?pubRef=-//EP//TEXT+TA+P7-TA-2011-0136+0+DOC+XML+V0//EN&language=EN
59. Council of the European Union (2011) Joint contribution of the German, French and United Kingdom delegations regarding the proposals for a directive laying down standards for the reception of asylum-seekers and for asylum procedures, 27 June 2011, 12168/11, para 5. Available via http://register.consilium.europa.eu/pdf/en/11/st12/st12168.en11.pdf
60. UNHCR (2003) Guidelines on International Protection No. 3: cessation of refugee status under Article 1C(5) and (6) of the 1951 Convention relating to the Status of Refugees (the "Ceased Circumstances" Clauses), 10 February 2003, HCR/GIP/03/03. Available via http://www.unhcr.org/refworld/docid/3e50de6b4.html
61. Achermann A, Gattiker M (1995) Safe third countries: European development. Int J Refugee Law 7(1):19–38
62. Baldaccini A, Guild E, Toner H (eds) (2007) Whose Freedom, Security and Justice?. Hart Publishing, Oxford
63. ECRE (1999) Guidelines on fair and efficient procedures for determining refugee status, brussels, ECRE, 1999. Available via http://www.ecre.org/resources/Policy_papers/233
64. Gil-Bazo MT (2006) The practice of mediterranean states in the context of the European Union's Justice and home affairs external dimension. The safe third country concept revisited. Int J Refugee Law 3(4):571–600
65. Gorta'zar C (2004) Asylum procedures. In: Dias Urbano De Sousa C, De Bruycker P (eds) The emergence of a European Asylum Policy. Bruylant, Brussels, pp 87–106
66. Ferguson Sidorenko O (2007) The common European asylum system: background, current state of affairs, future direction. T.M.C. ASSER Press, The Hague
67. Hailbronner K (1993) The concept of 'Safe Country' and expeditious asylum procedures: a Western European perspective. Int J Refugee Law 5(1):2–32
68. Kjaergaard E (1994) The concept of "Safe Third Country" in contemporary European refugee law. Int J Refugee Law 6(4):644–655
69. Kjaerum M (1992) The concept of country of first asylum. Int J Refugee Law 4(4):514–530
70. Morgades S (2010) The externalisation of the asylum function in the European union No. 4 Spring. GRITIM working Papers, University of Pompeu Fabra. Available via www.upf.edu/gritim, pp 9–10
71. El-Enany N (2008) Who is the new European refugee? Eur Law Rev 33(3):313–335
72. Gammeltoft-Hansen T (2010) The externalisation of European migration control and the reach of international refugee law. In: Guild E, Minderhoud P Cholewinski R (eds) The first decade of EU migration and asylum law. Martinus Nijhoff Publishers, Leiden, pp 273–298
73. Moreno-Lax V (2012) Hirsi Jamaa and others v Italy or the Strasbourg court versus extraterritorial migration control? Hum Rights Law Rev 12(3):574–598
74. Velluti S (2013) External aspects of EU asylum law and policy—new ways to address old woes. In: Abbas A, Ippolito F (eds) Regional approaches to the protection of asylum-seekers: an international legal perspective. Ashgate, Dartmouth (forthcoming)
75. EU Network of Independent Experts on Fundamental Rights (CFR-CDF) (2004) Thematic comment No. 2: fundamental rights in the external activities of the European union in the fields of justice and asylum and immigration in 2003. CFR-CDF.Them.Com.2003.en

76. ecre (2011) comments from the european council on refugees and exiles on the amended commission proposal to recast the reception conditions directive (com(2011) 320 final). Available via http://www.ecre.org/component/content/article/57-policy-papers/253-ecre-comments-and-recommendations-on-the-amended-commission-proposal-to-recast-the-reception-conditions-directive-com2011-320-final.html
77. Odysseus (2006) Comparative overview of the implementation of the directive 2003/9 of 27 January 2003 laying down minimum standards for the reception of asylum-seekers in the EU Member States, Academic network for legal studies on immigration and asylum in Europe. Available via http://ec.europa.eu/dgs/home-affairs/e-library/docs/pdf/odysseus_synthesis_report_2007_en_en.pdf
78. European Commission (2007) Report from the commission to the council and to the European parliament on the application of Directive 2003/9/EC of 27 January 2003 laying down minimum standards for the reception of asylum-seekers. COM(2007)745 final
79. European Commission (2008) Proposal for a directive of the European parliament and of the council laying down minimum standards for the reception of asylum-seekers (Recast), 3 December 2008, COM(2008) 815 final
80. UN Sub-Commission on the Promotion and Protection of Human Rights (2000) Resolution 2000/21 on the detention of asylum-seekers. Available via http://www.refworld.org/docid/3dda66394.html
81. UN Commission on Human Rights (1998) Report of the working group on arbitrary Detention: Addendum: report on the visit of the Working Group to the United Kingdom on the issue of immigrants and asylum-seekers, 18 December 1998, E/CN.4/1999/63/Add.3. Availablevia http://www.refworld.org/docid/45377b810.html
82. Council of Europe: Committee of Ministers (2003) Recommendation Rec (2003)5 of the Committee of ministers to member states on measures of detention of asylum-seekers. Available via http://www.refworld.org/docid/3f8d65e54.html
83. European Parliament (2009) European parliament legislative resolution of 7 May 2009 on the proposal for a directive of the European parliament and of the Council laying down minimum standards for the reception of asylum-seekers (Recast), P6_TA-PROV(2009)0376. Available via http://www.europarl.europa.eu/sides/getDoc.do?type=TA&language=EN&reference=P6-TA-2009-0376
84. European Commission (2011) Amended proposal for a directive of the European parliament and of the council laying down standards for the reception of asylum-seekers (Recast), 1 June 2011, COM(2011) 320 final. Available via http://eur-lex.europa.eu/LexUriServ/LexUriServ.do?uri=COM:2011:0320:FIN:EN:PDF
85. Jastram K, Newland K (2001) Family unity and refugee protection. Paper commissioned by UNHCR. Available via www.unhcr.org/3bd3d4a14.pdf
86. Hailbronner K (2007) Detention of asylum-seekers. Eur J Migr Law 9(2):159–172
87. O'Nions H (2008) No right to liberty: the detention of asylum-seekers for administrative convenience. Eur J Migr Law 10(2):149–185
88. Costello C (2012) Human rights and the elusive universal subject: immigration detention under international human rights and EU law. Indiana J Global Legal Stud 19(1):257–303
89. Amnesty International (2009) Amnesty International's Comments on the Commission Proposals for a Directive laying down Minimum Standards for the reception of asylum-seekers (Recast) (COM(2008) 815 final) and on the Commission Proposal for a Regulation establishing the criteria and mechanisms for determining the Member State responsible for examining an application for international protection lodged in one of the Member States by a third-country national or a stateless person (Recast) (COM(2008) 820 final), April 2009. Available via http://www.statewatch.org/news/2009/apr/ai-dublin-reception-aprl-2009.pdf, p. 4
90. Goodwin-Gill G (2003) Article 31 of the 1951 convention relating to the status of refugees: non-penalization, detention and protection. In: Feller E, Türk V, Nicholson F (eds) Refugee protection in international law: UNHCR's global consultations of international protection. CUP, Cambridge. Available via http://www.unhcr.org/4a1ba1aa6.html

91. UNHCR (1999) UNHCR's revised guidelines on applicable criteria and standards relating to the detention of asylum-seekers. Available via http://www.refworld.org/docid/3c2b3f844.html
92. UNHCR (2012) Guidelines on the applicable criteria and standards relating to the detention of asylum-seekers and alternatives to detention. Available via http://www.refworld.org/docid/503489533b8.html
93. European Committee for the Prevention of Torture and Inhuman or Degrading Treatment or Punishment (CPT) (2002) Standards, CPT/Inf/E/(2002) 1—Rev. 2010, para 28. Available via http://www.cpt.coe.int
94. Smyth C (2013) Is the right of the child to liberty safeguarded in the common European asylum system? Eur J Migr Law 15(2):111–136
95. Wisher D (2009) The liberty of foreigners: A History, law and politics of immigration detention. Wolf Legal Publishers, Nijmegen
96. Cornelisse G (2011) Detention of foreigners. In: Guild E Minderhoud P, Cholewinski R (eds) The first decade of EU migration and asylum law. Martinus Nijhoff Publishers, Leiden, pp 207–226
97. della Cananea G (2003) Beyond the State: the Europeanization and globalization of procedural administrative Law. Eur Public Law 9(4):563–577
98. Schwarze J (2000) The convergence of the administrative laws of The EU member states. In; Snyder F (ed) The Europeanization of law: the legal effects of European integration. Hart, Oxford, pp 163–182
99. Beck RJ (1999) Britain and the 1933 refugee convention: national or state sovereignty? Int J Refugee Law 11:597–624
100. Joppke C (1997) Asylum and state sovereignty: a comparison of the United States, Germany and Britain. Comp Political Stud 30(3):259–298
101. Walker (2003) Late sovereignty in the European Union. In: Walker N (ed) Sovereignty in Transition. Hart, Oxford, pp 3–32
102. Werner WG, De Wilde JH (2001) The endurance of sovereignty. Eur J Int Relat 7(3):283–313
103. Alter KJ (2009) The European court's political power. OUP, Oxford
104. Garrett G, Kelemen RD, Schulz H (1998) The European court of justice, national governments, and legal integration in the European Union. Int Organ 52(1):149–176
105. Stone Sweet A (2010) The European court of justice and the judicialization of EU governance. Living reviews in EU governance. Yale Law School. Available via http://digitalcommons.law.yale.edu/cgi/viewcontent.cgi?article=1069&context=fss_papers
106. Council of Europe (2010) The conscience of Europe. 50 Years of the European court of human rights. Third Millennium Publishing, London
107. Mowbray A (2004) The development of positive obligations under the European convention on human rights by the European court of human rights. Hart, Oxford
108. Viljanen J (2008) The role of the European court of human rights as a developer of international human rights law. Cuadernos Constitucionales de la Cátedra Fadrique Furió Ceriol no 62/63. Pp. 249–265
109. Neuman G (2003) Human rights and constitutional rights: harmony and dissonance. Stanford Law Rev 55:1863–1900
110. Slaughter A-M, Burke-White W (2006) The future of international law is domestic (or, The European Way of Law). Harvard Int Law J 47(2):327–352

Chapter 4
The Role of the European Courts in Ensuring Adequate Standards of Asylum-Seekers' Human Rights' Protection in Europe After Lisbon

4.1 The European Court of Human Rights and the European Court of Justice as "Regional Refugee Law Courts"

On the basis of a comparative analysis of a series of key asylum cases (most of which decided around the time of or after the entry into force of the ToL), this section seeks to critically examine the jurisprudence of the ECJ and the ECtHR in the field of asylum *vis-à-vis* the ECHR and the EU Charter, in consideration of the fact that in Europe these two courts have gradually established themselves as the two key "regional refugee law courts." The focus of analysis is centred on the complex and evolving constitutional relationship between the EU and the overall system of the ECHR in order to assess the standard of asylum-seekers' fundamental rights protection in Europe. In particular, it examines the legality of and compatibility with the ECHR and the EU Charter of the main legislative instruments of CEAS—prior to their reform-such as, for example, the Dublin II regulation, the Qualification, Asylum Procedures and the Reception Conditions Directives. This jurisprudential analysis is particularly necessary in consideration of the fact that a comparison between the first and the second legislative phase of CEAS shows that, despite experiencing a major change in its institutional dimension, EU asylum law carries on displaying a significant degree of continuity substantively.[1]

With regard to the actual use of the ECHR made by the ECJ, former AG Jacobs maintains that 'the European Court of Justice has treated [...] the European Convention on Human Rights as if it were binding upon the Community, and has

Many of the ideas developed in this section are the result of collaborative research with Dr Ippolito conducted during my Visiting Professorship at the University of Cagliari, School of Law, Italy (March–August 2012).

[1] See Ref. [1] who demonstrate how institutional change does not necessarily trigger policy change.

S. Velluti, *Reforming the Common European Asylum System - Legislative Developments and Judicial Activism of the European Courts*, SpringerBriefs in Law,
DOI: 10.1007/978-3-642-40267-8_4, © The Author(s) 2014

followed scrupulously the case-law of the European Court of Human Rights, even though the European Union itself is not a party to the Convention.'[2] While a close examination of the ECJ's case law confirms that the Luxembourg Court has never openly contradicted or departed from the Strasbourg Court's rulings and that similarly the ECtHR in cases concerning the EU legal order has shown almost a deferential approach—most notoriously with the *Bosphorus* presumption-[3] it is also equally true that there has been an incoherent or piecemeal use of the ECHR and the Strasbourg case-law by the ECJ, which in turn is reflected in the way the ECtHR has been using the case-law of the ECJ.[4] Furthermore, while Article 52(3) of the EU Charter sheds some light on the content of EU fundamental rights *vis-à-vis* Convention rights it remains silent as regards the relationship of the EU Charter with the jurisprudence of the ECtHR, leaving the problem of the two-court system unresolved.

To date, the Luxembourg and Strasbourg Courts have resolved their collisions and conflicts in an informal setting of cross-fertilization and mutual acknowledgment[5] as confirmed by the Joint Communication of the Presidents Costa and Skouris,[6] which has been defined as a kind of "common supranational diplomacy."[7] Beyond any definition, this type of arrangement is meant to maintain the autonomy and primacy of the ECJ within the EU system. In *Kamberaj*,[8] the ECJ referred to the distinctiveness of the two European human rights regimes by stating that Article 6(3) TEU[9] does not lead to a progressive incorporation of the ECHR into EU law or to the extension of the principles of primacy and direct effect to the ECHR by virtue of this provision. Once again, the Luxembourg Court seems driven by a concern to preserve the autonomy of the EU legal order.[10] It is here posited that it is precisely this concern over the autonomy and distinctiveness of the EU legal system coupled with elements of classical sovereignty, chiefly territoriality, found in certain cases of the ECtHR concerning asylum (such as

---

[2] See Ref. [2], p. 54.

[3] This important concept is examined in the next section.

[4] See Refs. [3–6]

[5] See S. Iglesias Sánchez (2012), footnote 136 in Ref. Chap. 2; see also [7]

[6] See Ref. [8].

[7] See Ref. [9].

[8] See Case C-571/10, *Servet Kamberaj v Istituto per l'Edilizia sociale della Provincia autonoma di Bolzano (IPES) and Others*, Judgment of the Court (Grand Chamber) of 24 April 2012, nyr, at paras 62–63.

[9] Article 6(3) TEU provides that: 'Fundamental rights, as guaranteed by the European Convention for the Protection of Human Rights and Fundamental Freedoms and as they result from the constitutional traditions common to the Member States, shall constitute general principles of the Union's law.'

[10] The autonomy of the Union's legal system has been most notoriously emphasized in the Kadi ruling, see Joined Cases C-402/05 P and C-415/05 P *Yassin Abdullah Kadi and Al Barakaat International Foundation v Council of the European Union and Commission of the European Communities* [2008] ECR I-6351.

detention) that is particularly problematic from the viewpoint of asylum-seekers' human rights protection. With this in mind the investigation, therefore, also intends to consider the extent to which the latter may hinder access to effective judicial remedies for asylum-seekers.

4.2 The European Court of Human Rights and Asylum

The preceding chapter showed that, while some significant steps forward have been made, problems remain for an effective protection of asylum-seekers' fundamental rights in Europe. In particular, the reform of key legislative instruments of CEAS has not adequately addressed the limitations of EU asylum legislation of CEAS' first phase. As Costello observes 'CEAS enshrines more mutual recognition of negative than positive decisions. The recognition of an asylum-seeker as a refugee in one Member State does not create EU obligations for the others. [...] Member States use mutual recognition as a selective tool, to limit responsibility, rather than to share it.'[11] As a consequence, the ECtHR has not refrained itself from adopting a more interventionist role in acting as a guarantor of human rights within the State Parties to its conventional regime as confirmed by the *MSS* judgment, examined further below.

The ECHR does not provide for a clear set of asylum-seekers' rights. However, the ECtHR has developed the bulk of its asylum jurisprudence on the basis of Article 3 ECHR,[12] particularly in relation to deportation and expulsion cases. In *Salah Sheekh* the Strasbourg Court emphasized the centrality and absolute nature of Article 3 ECHR stating that it enshrines one of the fundamental values of democratic societies and prohibits in absolute terms torture or inhuman or degrading treatment or punishment, irrespective of the victim's conduct, however undesirable or dangerous. It then held that in exercising their right to expel individuals, Contracting States must take into due consideration Article 3 ECHR

[11] See Ref. [10], at 335.

[12] Asylum cases also concern other Convention rights. Specifically, Article 2 ECHR (right to life), Article 4 ECHR (prohibition of slavery, servitude, and compulsory labour), Article 5 ECHR (right to liberty and security of the person), Article 6 ECHR (right to a fair trial), Article 7 ECHR (prohibition on retroactive criminal punishment), Article 8 ECHR (right to respect for family and private life), Article 9 ECHR (right to freedom of thought, conscience, and religion), Article 10 ECHR (freedom of expression), Article 11 ECHR (freedom of assembly and association), Article 13 ECHR (right to an effective remedy), Article 14 ECHR (prohibition of discrimination in the enjoyment of Convention rights), Article 4 of Protocol No. 4 (collective expulsion of aliens), Article 1 of Protocol No. 7 (procedural safeguards relating to expulsion of aliens), Article 3 of Protocol No. 7 (exclusion of own nationals), Article 4 of Protocol No. 7 (prohibition on double jeopardy), Article 1 of Protocol No. 12 (general prohibition on discrimination); see further Refs. [11, 12]; Council of Europe and European Union Agency for Fundamental Rights (2013), *Handbook on European Law relating to asylum, borders and immigration* (Luxembourg: Publications Office of the European Union); on Article 13 ECHR and asylum, see Ref. [13].

and thus the expulsion of an alien may give rise to an issue under this provision and engage the responsibility of the expelling State under the Convention, where substantial grounds have been shown for believing that the person in question, if expelled, would face a real risk of being subjected to treatment contrary to Article 3 ECHR in the receiving country. In such circumstances, Article 3 ECHR implies an obligation not to expel the individual to that country, namely the principle of *non-refoulement.*[13]

Moving to the compliance of EU law with the European Convention, the initial position was that a direct control over EU primary law was inadmissible *ratione personae* as the then European Community (EC) was not a party to the ECHR.[14] Such direct control has been subsequently declared admissible in relation to those primary EC treaties over which the ECJ had no jurisdiction.[15] In cases where the Strasbourg Court was called to assess Member States' responsibility *ratione materiae* it developed the notion of presumption of "equivalent protection", namely, that under EU law fundamental rights are protected in a way which could be considered "equivalent" to that provided for by the Convention.[16] This concept was fully developed in the well-known case of *Bosphorus*[17] where the concept of "equivalency" (of protection under EU law) was associated with that of "comparable" (rather than identical level) of protection of human rights. Linked to the latter, it also went on to develop the other equally important notion of "presumption of conventionality," namely, once it is demonstrated that an equivalent protection is provided within an international organization, the presumption will

[13] See e.g. *Salah Sheekh v. the Netherlands,* Application No. 1948/04, judgment of 11 January 2007 at para 135; *Cruz Varas and others v. Sweden,* Application No. 15576/89, judgment of 20 March 1991; *Vilvarajah and others v. the United Kingdom,* Application nos. 13163/87, 13164/87 and 13165/87, judgment of 30 October 1991; *Chahal v. the United Kingdom,* Application No. 22414/93, judgment of 15 November 1996 and *Amuur v. France,* Application No. 19776/92, judgment of 25 June 1996; *Saadi v. Italy,* Application No. 37201/06, judgment of 28 February 2008.

[14] As held by the former European Commission of Human Rights in *CFDT v European Community*, Application 8030/77, decision of 10 July 1978. EU accession to the ECHR is beyond the scope of this investigation. It has been debated and examined for over 30 years and is well-documented, see e.g. Article 6(2) TEU, Protocol (No. 8) relating to Article 6(2) of the Treaty on European Union on the Accession of the Union to the European Convention on the Protection of Human Rights and Fundamental Freedoms, [2007] OJ C306/155; Protocol 14 to the European Convention of Human Rights and Fundamental Freedoms, amending the Control System of the Convention, of 13 May 2004, ETS 194, specifically Article 59(2) ECHR in order to allow a non-state entity such as the EU to accede to the ECHR; [38]; [14–18]. For further information, visit the Council of Europe dedicated webpage on EU accession, http://hub.coe.int/what-we-do/human-rights/eu-accession-to-the-convention.

[15] See e.g. *Matthews v United Kingdom,* Application No. 24833/94, Judgment of 18 February 1999, at paras 32–33.

[16] See e.g. *M & Co. v. Federal Republic of Germany*, Application No. 13258/87, Decision of 9 February 1990.

[17] See *Bosphorus v. Ireland*, (Application N° 45036/98), Judgment of 30 June 2005, at paras 155–157.

be that a country has not departed from the requirements of the ECHR when it does no more than implement legal obligations flowing from its membership of the organization. It follows that if a Member State has no discretion in implementing the legal obligations deriving from its membership of the organization it will not be found responsible for the acts and omissions of the international organization to which it has conferred powers. Such presumption can be rebutted on the basis that protection in a particular case may be regarded as "manifestly deficient." As to EU asylum law, the Strasbourg Court has been called to decide on a number of cases concerning the Dublin system. Its initial position has been that in the context of such system there is a presumption that each Member State will comply with the Asylum Procedures and the Reception Conditions Directives in order to guarantee for minimum standards in asylum procedures and reception conditions for asylum-seekers.[18]

However, this presumption was considered rebutted for the first time in the landmark *MSS* ruling concerning an Afghan asylum-seeker who was returned by Belgium to Greece under the Dublin II Regulation.[19] The Strasbourg Court held that there should be a proper *ad hoc* assessment every time there is a serious doubt for the sending State that the Asylum Procedures and Reception Directives are not being implemented effectively in the destination State to the extent that there are "major structural deficiencies" in the asylum procedure and reception conditions for asylum applicants, which result in inhuman or degrading treatment.[20] The Strasbourg Court gave considerable weight to a series of reports published since 2006 by the Council of Europe, the EU, the UNHCR and NGOs.[21] Moreover, the ECtHR not long before the delivery of its judgment in *MSS*, had found degrading detention conditions in three cases against Greece.[22] According to Maiani and Hruschka,[23] the Court itself in examining the situation in Greece drew a distinction between the "Sollen," that is, what is provided by national law and the "Sein", that is, the actual situation on the ground.

The presumption upon which the CEAS was based was no longer considered *per se* a sufficient basis for intra-EU transfers of asylum-seekers and the ECtHR

---

[18] See *K.R.S. v. United Kingdom*, Application no. 32733/08, 2 December 2008, where the ECtHR held that the system so created 'protects fundamental rights, as regards both the substantive guarantees offered and the mechanisms controlling their observance.'

[19] See *MSS v Belgium and Greece*, Application No. 30696/09, Judgment 21 January 2011. Space precludes an exhaustive review of this landmark ruling, for case comment and critical analysis, see Ref. [19]; Maiani and Hruschka (2011), see footnote 8 in Chap. 3 [20, 21].

[20] See *MSS,* at para 300.

[21] See *MSS*, para 160.

[22] See *SD v Greece*, Application No. 53541/07, Judgment of 11 June 2009; *Tabesh v Greece*, Application No. 8256/07, Judgment of 26 November 2009; *AA v Greece*, Application No. 12186/08, Judgment of 22 July 2010.

[23] See Maiani and Hruschka (2011), see footnote 8 in Chap. 3, at 15, who write: 'la Cour fait méticuleusement la différence entre le *Sollen*-ce qui est prévu par la législation nationale-et le *Sein*-la situation sur le terrain.'

held that the practical implementation of protection standards by the Member State concerned must be considered. The protection of human rights in the EU—and chiefly the protection against indirect *refoulement*-[24] was ensured by the Court on the basis of a derogation clause *as per* Article 3(2) of the Dublin II Regulation.[25] Hence, it may be argued that following *MSS.* The clause has been re-conceptualized from being a mere residual guarantee of Member States' sovereignty to a necessary guarantee for ensuring compliance with EU and International human rights law.[26] In addition, the Strasbourg Court stressed the need for a 'comprehensive reconsideration of the existing European legal regime.'[27] Significantly, EU asylum standards set out in the EU Procedures and Reception Directives have been used by the ECtHR in order to identify the lack of adequate protection *beyond* the traditional Conventional rights and, specifically, to extend the notion of inhuman and degrading treatment to "living conditions" of asylum-seekers, such as destitution and poverty,[28] the 'particularly serious' deprivation of material reception conditions (including accommodation, food and clothing, in kind or in the form of monetary allowances) sufficient to protect the asylum-seekers. In *MSS*, failure by Greece to comply with the Reception Directive influenced the Court's reasoning and it was used as an aggravating factor.[29]

However, when the ECtHR was called to consider the deprivation of benefits to which the applicant was entitled to under the Qualification Directive, the Court stated that it was not its task to apply directly the level of protection offered in other international instruments.[30] In *Ahmed v the United Kingdom* the authorities had refused the applicant's claim for asylum and his appeal rights were exhausted. However, further to his complaint to the Court the impending removal to Somalia was lifted. Subsequently, he sought compensation, *inter alia,* on the basis that he

---

[24] The *non-refoulement* obligation under Article 3 ECHR includes also the so-called "indirect" *refoulement* which entails return to a country from where there is a risk of onward return to ill-treatment, see *T.I. v. United Kingdom*, Appl. No. 43844/98, 7 March 2000, p. 15; see also *Salah Sheekh v. The Netherlands*, 11 Jan. 2007, para 141; in *K.R.S. v. UK,* Application No. 32733/08, admissibility decision, 2 Dec. 2008, p. 16; and in *Abdolkhani and Karimnia v. Turkey*, Appl. No. 30471/08, 22 Sept. 2009, at paras 88–89.

[25] Now Article 17(1) of the Dublin III Regulation.

[26] This is an observation made by Ippolito [39].

[27] The Court stressed how such a needed on-going reform process of the CEAS' instruments was aimed in particular, 'at substantially strengthening the protection of the fundamental rights of asylum-seekers implementing a temporary suspension of transfers under the Dublin Regulation to avoid asylum-seekers being sent back to Member States unable to offer them a sufficient level of protection of their fundamental rights' (at para 350).

[28] See para 250; see also *Budina v. Russia,* Application No. 45603/05.

[29] See Ref. [22], at 768.

[30] See *Ahmed v. the United Kingdom* Application No. 31668/05, decision (inadmissible*);* see also *N.A. v. the United Kingdom,* Application No. 25904/07 judgment of 17 July 2008, where the ECtHR already held that its supervisory role under Article 19 was confined to examining alleged breaches of provisions of the ECHR (e.g. in that case, Article 3) and therefore any submissions on EU asylum law (concerning the Qualification Directive) fell outside its jurisdiction.

had been deprived of the benefits of access to employment, welfare payments and accommodation to which he would have been entitled if his claim under the Qualification Directive had been recognized. The Court stated that it was not necessary to provide redress for any pecuniary or non-pecuniary damage incurred by the applicant while he was under threat of removal to Somalia. Specifically, it was not for the Court to apply directly the level of protection offered in other international instruments and consequently held that the applicant's submissions based on the Directive were outside the scope of its examination of the present application.

In addition and linked to this, in *Sufi and Elmi* the ECtHR made it clear that it was inappropriate for the Court to decide on the scope of EU law.[31] It did state though that Article 3 ECHR offered "comparable protection" to that afforded under the then Article 15 (c) of the Qualification Directive as interpreted by the ECJ in *Elgafaji*.[32] In particular, according to the Strasbourg judges, 'the threshold set by both provisions may, in exceptional circumstances, be attained in consequence of a situation of general violence of such intensity that any person being returned to the region in question would be at risk simply on account of their presence there.' As noted by Ippolito 'the identification by the ECtHR in *Sufi and Elmi* of some specific (non-exhaustive) criteria for assessing the level of severity of a situation of general violence which is necessary to reach the threshold of a *"real risk"*[33] may provide guidance for the assessment of applications for subsidiary protection as well as impact on the future application of the *Elgafaji*'s principle by domestic courts.'[34] In *Hirsi*[35] the ECtHR referred to the EU Charter in declaring Italy's responsibility for failure to fulfill its international refugee law obligations and highlighted that the *non-refoulement* principle is also enshrined in Article 19 of the EU Charter.[36] The judgment was the first one on interception-at-sea, which established some important new legal principles on collective expulsions under Article 4 of Protocol 4.[37] Indeed, the ECtHR for the first time applied

[31] See *Sufi and Elmi v United Kingdom,* Applications nos. 8319/07 and 11449/07, paras 225–226.

[32] See C-465/07 *Elgafaji and Elgafaji v Staatssecretaris van Justitie* ECR [2009] I-921.

[33] See *Sufi and Elmi v United Kingdom,* para 241.

[34] See Ippolito, in Ippolito and Velluti (2014), see footnote 26.

[35] See *Hirsi Jamaa and Others v Italy,* Application No. 27765/09, 23 February 2012. For critical analysis and case comment, see Ref. [23].

[36] The Court also considered the information provided by Mr Jacques Barrot, Vice-President of European Commission in a letter dated 15 May 2009 sent to the President of the European Parliament Committee on Civil Liberties, Justice and Home Affairs in response to a request for a legal opinion on the 'return to Libya by sea of various groups of migrants by the Italian authorities.' In the letter he stressed the importance of compliance with the principle of *non-refoulement* in the context of operations carried out on the high seas by Member States of the European Union; see *Hirsi,* at paras 135 with 34.

[37] Unanimously, the Grand Chamber found a violation of Article 3 ECHR prohibiting inhuman and degrading treatment on a double count (risk of ill-treatment in Libya and risk of repatriation from Libya to countries where there is a risk of ill-treatment), a violation of Article 4 of Protocol

this provision extraterritorially. In *Hirsi* the Strasbourg Court followed its approach developed earlier in *MSS* in relation to the burden of proof placed upon the applicant. In particular, by departing from its position in *Vilvarajah*,[38] it stated that there is no need to provide evidence of an individualized threat of torture or other proscribed ill-treatment for Article 3 ECHR to be engaged. What is pivotal is the country's information contained in reports from independent sources,[39] providing reliable accounts of the circumstances prevailing in the receiving state make it "sufficiently real and probable" that the general situation may entail risks for the individual as per Article 3 ECHR, the removal must be suspended.[40] In addition the state concerned must proactively implement its Article 3 obligations and undertake the relevant investigation *proprio motu*. Furthermore, a presumption of safety based solely on enacted domestic legislation and ratification of international human rights instruments by the third country in question does not constitute a sufficient guarantee of effective protection on the ground. It follows that the contracting state in question is not released from its obligations under the ECHR. What is required rather is an evaluation of whether those obligations are actually being implemented in practice.

With regard to immigration detention, Article 5(1)(f) ECHR on the right to personal liberty and security only recognizes two legitimate aims for detaining foreigners in immigration procedures: the prevention of unlawful entries and effectuating deportations. It follows that detention in cases where deportation is not possible or where it is used as a deterrent is unlawful under Article 5(1)(f) ECHR. The lawfulness of a decision to detain an alien will be assessed in relation to four aspects of the detention, namely, the quality of the national laws authorizing the detention; the conditions and place of detention; the underlying aim of the detention; and the duration of the detention.[41] In *Chahal*, when reviewing the initial decision by the state to detain somebody who is to be deported, it stated that 'Article 5(1)(f) does not demand that the detention of a person against whom action is being taken with a view to deportation be reasonably considered necessary, for example to prevent his committing an offence or fleeing; in this respect Article 5(1)(f) provides a different level of protection from Article 5(1)(c). Indeed, all that is required under this provision is that action is being taken with a view to deportation'. It may be inferred that according to the Court under Article 5(1)(f) it is irrelevant whether the underlying decision to expel can be justified under national or Convention law.[42]

(Footnote 37 continued)
No. 4 prohibiting collective expulsion and a violation of Article 13 ECHR guaranteeing a domestic remedy for any arguable complaint of a violation of the Convention.

[38] See *Vilvarajah and Others v United Kingdom* Application nos. 13163/87, 13164/87 and 13165/87, Judgment of 30 October 1991.

[39] See *Hirsi*, at paras. 118 and 123.

[40] Ibidem, at para 136.

[41] For critical commentary and a detailed list of cases of the ECtHR, see Costello (2012), see footnote 177 in Chap. 3, at 278–281.

[42] See *Chahal v. the United Kingdom*, at para 112.

In *Čonka*, the Court re-stated that an unnecessary pre-deportation detention does not constitute an unlawful detention.[43] In so doing, it may be argued that it endorsed interferences with the right to personal liberty that are unnecessary. This approach is unhelpful towards unwanted migrants and may seriously undermine the protection of their right to personal liberty. This is unless national laws put down a necessity requirement, as the detention has to be in accordance with national law as in *Rusu*[44] where the detention was deemed arbitrary precisely for failure to comply with the Austrian domestic legal standards and specifically the necessity test.[45]

In *Saadi*,[46] the Court adopted a similar approach. This is the leading case on detention as a measure to prevent unauthorized entry. Notably, it was a case that divided the judges and the partly dissenting opinion of Judges Rozakis, Tulkens, Kovler, Hajiyev, Spielmann, and Hirvela deserves mention because it provides important counter-arguments to the view taken by the majority of the Grand Chamber. Saadi was a Kurdish national from Iraq, who applied for asylum in the United Kingdom. After a few days, during which he was granted temporary leave to remain, he was detained in a centre that was specifically designed to hold asylum-seekers while their claims where decided in a fast track procedure to ensure speedy and efficient decision-making. The Court held by majority that 'the principle that detention should not be arbitrary must apply to detention under the first limb of Article 5(1)(f) in the same manner as it applies to detention under the second limb. Since *States enjoy the right to control equally an alien's entry into and residence in their country*, it would be artificial to apply a different proportionality test to cases of detention at the point of entry than that which applies to deportation, extradition or expulsion of a person already in the country.'[47] Consequently, as in the case of pre-deportation, pre-admittance detention must not be a necessary measure. In this context, Costello talks about detention becoming the "necessary adjunct" to state territoriality and, in particular, to sovereign entry control which 'imports the statist assumption into detention practices.'[48] At the same time, in *Saadi* the ECtHR laid out four requirements to prevent arbitrariness in detention. In particular, detention must be[49]:

(1) carried out in good faith;
(2) closely connected to the purpose of preventing unauthorized entry of the person;

---

[43] See *Čonka v. Belgium*, at para 38.

[44] See Cornelisse (2011), see footnote 95 in Chap. 2, at p. 214.

[45] The notion of "arbitrariness" includes elements of inappropriateness, injustice, lack of predictability and due process of law.

[46] See *Saadi v United Kingdom* (Grand Chamber), 29 January 2008, Application No. 13229/03.

[47] Ibidem, at para 73. Emphasis added.

[48] See Costello (2012), see footnote 177 in Chap. 3, at 283.

[49] See *Saadi v United Kingdom*, at para 74.

(3) in an appropriate place and under appropriate conditions bearing in mind that detainee has not "committed criminal offences" but rather may have fled fearing for his life; and
(4) the length of the detention should not exceed that reasonably required for the purpose pursued.

Applying these criteria to Saadi's detention, as the purpose of the deprivation of liberty was to enable the authorities to determine in an expedite and efficient manner the applicant's claim to asylum, that requirement was considered to be satisfied. The issues concerning the necessity and the proportionality of the detention were only considered in relation to the duration of the detention.[50] In *Saadi*, the Court held that 7 days spent in detention by Saadi was not excessive, in view of the purpose, namely speedy decision making in the asylum procedure, and in consideration of the fact that at the time of the detention the United Kingdom faced administrative difficulties.[51]

The dissenting judges criticized the majority's approach on a number of issues. In particular, they noted that the majority failed to distinguish between different categories of migrants, subjecting them all to the 'states' unlimited sovereignty.'[52] As regards the application of the criteria to the facts of the *Saadi* case, they took the view that the majority's approach to the duration of detention gave ample discretion to states as to what is an acceptable duration of lawful detention.[53] Significantly, the dissenting judges also exposed the limitations of the majority's approach from the perspective of international human rights. In particular, they noted that the 'ECHR 'does not apply in a vacuum,'[54] and mentioned the key Human Rights Committee (HRC) jurisprudence and EU norms, noting that Article 18(1) of the Asylum Procedures Directive, precluding detention for the "sole reason" of being a refugee, should be regarded as "the minimum guarantee."[55]

Criticisms to the *Saadi* decision were also made by the Council of Europe's Parliamentary Assembly in relation to the interpretation of "unauthorized entry" as *de facto* it enabled states to detain without limitation and more generally as it was found to be in "blatant conflict" with the UNHCR guidelines on detention in allowing detention throughout the entire asylum process.[56]

---

[50] In *Chahal* the Court stated that deprivation of liberty will be justified only as long as deportation proceedings are in progress and if these proceedings are not carried out with due diligence, the detention will cease to be lawful under Article 5, see *Chahal v. the United Kingdom*, at para 113.

[51] See *Saadi v United Kingdom*, at para 79.

[52] Ibidem, at para 32.

[53] Ibidem, at para 34.

[54] Ibidem, at para 34.

[55] Ibidem, at paras 34–35.

[56] See Ref. [24]; see also the Explanatory Memorandum to the same document by the Rapporteur Mendonça, available at: http://assembly.coe.int/ASP/Doc/XrefViewHTML.asp?FileID=12435&Language=EN.

In *Lokpo and Touré v. Hungary*,[57] the ECtHR held that the detention of the applicants for a 5 month period for the purposes of removal which never materialized was disproportionate to the aim of removal pursued by the state. In particular, the detention of asylum-seekers was deemed unlawful due to the authority's failure to make a reasoned decision to continue detention: "non-action" or "mere silence" in the continued detention was deemed insufficient to meet the requirement of legality.[58] Regrettably, the ECtHR did not engage with the compatibility of domestic law with EU asylum law standards even though the legislation concerned had been enacted to implement the Asylum Procedures Directive.

The detention cases examined above question the level of protection offered by the ECtHR, particularly in view of its recurring statement that any deprivation of liberty should be in accordance with the general principles expressed or implied in the Convention.[59] The reason for the Court's inadequate protection for immigration detainees and for the granting to states of an almost unlimited margin of appreciation in deciding on immigration detention is not only explained by an uneasiness to encroach too far on an area that consists of "high politics" but also because of the persistence of the unchallenged idea of territoriality.[60]

Undoubtedly, what transpires from the analysis of the Strasbourg Court's decisions is that EU asylum law is gradually becoming increasingly important in the ECtHR's asylum case-law[61] and may well-exemplify what Callewaert defines as the "unionisation" of the Convention,[62] although it is difficult to define it in exact terms. Moreover, what the foregoing analysis already seems to suggest is that both European Courts are being influenced by each other's decisions whilst at the same time respecting the distinctiveness of the two European systems. One exception to this evolution is the area of immigration detention where the ECtHR'a case-law is seriously lacking in considerations of proportionality and necessity, although they are not completely absent from its judgments.

4.3 The European Court of Justice and Asylum

The ECJ has progressively asserted itself as "fundamental rights' court."[63] In so doing, it has attributed "special significance" to the ECHR in the EU legal order and it has relied on Convention rights as providing minimum standards for

[57] See *Lokpo and Touré v. Hungary*, Application No. 10816/10, Judgment of 20 September 2011.

[58] See *Lokpo and Touré*, paras 23–24.

[59] See Cornelisse, see footnote 198 in Chap. 3, at p. 215.

[60] Ibidem, at p. 215 and 220.

[61] See Ippolito, in Ippolito and Velluti (2014), see footnote 26.

[62] See Ref. [25].

[63] See Ref. [26]

developing EU fundamental rights.[64] With the legally binding status acquired by the EU Charter following the entry into force of the ToL, a question that arises is how this alters the approach of the ECJ towards the European Convention[65] and the jurisprudence of the ECtHR, which is particularly prominent in the context of asylum where, as we have seen in the preceding section, the Strasbourg Court has given important decisions. Article 52(3) of the EU Charter answers only partially this question as it is not of much aid in cases where the content of the rights is or may not be identical. To a certain extent, as this section will go on to show, the ECJ clearly intends to interpret EU asylum legislation in a manner which is consistent with the ECtHR asylum jurisprudence. On the other hand, the Luxembourg Court is also concerned with preserving the autonomy of its own jurisdiction and, more broadly, the EU legal order and the EU Charter is thus becoming a vehicle for expanding the scope of protection of "EU" fundamental rights. In this context, it will not refrain itself from adopting a more "progressive" approach in interpreting relevant provisions to ensure this end.

Elgafaji,[66] one of the first important ECJ cases concerning EU asylum law, exemplifies an hermeneutic approach of the Court which favors an autonomous interpretation of EU law, namely, one which does not rely on ECHR provisions to outline and develop the actual content of EU asylum Directives' provisions. In the words of Ippolito, 'the Court referred to the ECHR and its case law, although mostly confirmatory of an EU fundamental right or principle determined through an *autonomous* interpretation of EU law.'[67] The case concerned the scope of subsidiary protection under Article 15(c) of the Qualification Directive following a referral of the Dutch Council of State. The latter asked the Court whether Article 15(c) offered supplementary protection compared to Article 3 ECHR and, if so, what the criteria were for determining that subsidiary protection should be granted. While both the Advocate General and the Court adopted an autonomous interpretation the manner in which they conceived it differed. According to AG Maduro, this "independent interpretation" of EU provisions was made necessary by the fact that it was not left to the ECJ to establish which of the dynamic

[64] In this sense, see Article 52(3) of the EU Charter which provides that in so far as it contains fundamental rights that correspond to those provided by the ECHR, the meaning and scope of the EU Charter's rights shall be the same as those of the ECHR rights. Hence, the meaning and scope of those fundamental rights that are already guaranteed by the ECHR must necessarily comprise the ECtHR jurisprudence. However, Article 52(3) of the EU Charter does not prevent Union law from providing more extensive protection and consequently the ECHR constitutes a "floor" rather than a "ceiling" for EU human rights law; see further Refs. [27, 28];

[65] In a similar vein, see Weiss (2011), see footnote 64, who argues that the ToL has brought challenges to the substance and methodology of human rights protection in the EU.

[66] See C-465/07 *Elgafaji and Elgafaji v Staatssecretaris van Justitie* ECR [2009] I-921; see also Ref. [29]

[67] See Ippolito in Ippolito and Velluti (2014), see footnote 26 in this chapter.

interpretations of Article 3 ECHR proposed by the ECtHR should prevail.[68] The ECJ adopted a different approach and started by reformulating the reference made by the national court. It then argued that Article 15(c) of the Directive was a provision, the content of which is different from that of Article 3 ECHR.[69] It followed that its interpretation 'must be carried out independently.' More specifically, with regard to the definition of "individual threat" the ECJ held that it would be violated where substantial grounds were shown for believing that a civilian, returned to the relevant country, would, solely on account of his presence on the territory of that country or region, face a real risk of being subjected to a threat of serious harm.[70] The Court further held that in order to demonstrate such a risk the applicant is not required to adduce evidence that he would be specifically targeted by reason of factors particular to his personal circumstances.[71] Be that as it may, the ECJ considered that such a situation would be "exceptional" in the context of such a high level of indiscriminate violence, concerning civilians coming from territories of armed conflict from which refuge is sought.[72] The more the applicant could show that he was specifically affected by factors particular to his personal circumstances, the lower the level of indiscriminate violence required for him to be eligible for subsidiary protection.[73] Significantly, the ECJ only made a reference to the ECtHR in an *obiter dictum* and, specifically, the case of *NA v United Kingdom*,[74] in order to confirm that the right to subsidiary protection autonomously interpreted was in line with ECHR rights and the ECtHR jurisprudence.[75]

Samba Diouf,[76] is another case in which the ECJ used an autonomous interpretation of EU law and, in so doing, it relied solely on the EU Charter. The case

---

[68] See *Elgafaji*, Opinion AG Maduro, at para 20.

[69] The Court stated that: 'it is [...] Article 15(b) which corresponds, in essence, to Article 3 of the ECHR,' while Article 15(c) covers "more general risks of harm" than the "particular ones" Article 15(a) requires the applicant to be "specifically exposed', see *Elgafaji*, at para 28.

[70] See *Elgafaji*, at para 43.

[71] Ibidem, at para 35.

[72] Ibidem, at para 39.

[73] Idem.

[74] See *NA v. the United Kingdom*, Application No. 25904/07, at para 115. In this case the ECtHR expressly considered its previous decision in *Vilvarajah* (Application Nos. 13163/87, 13164/87, 13165/87, 13447/87, 13448/87) and stated that Article 3 ECHR should not be interpreted so as to require an applicant to show the existence of special distinguishing features if he could otherwise show that the general situation of violence in the country of destination was of a sufficient level of intensity to create a real risk that any removal to that country would violate Article 3 ECHR. In any event, the Court would adopt such an approach only in the most extreme cases of general violence where there was a real risk of ill-treatment simply by virtue of an individual being exposed to such violence on return; see also *F.H. v. Sweden* (Application no. 32621/06, 20 January 2009, at para 93 and *Mawaka v. The Netherlands*, Application no. 29031/04, 1 June 2010.

[75] See *Elgafaji*, at para 44.

[76] See Case C-69/10 *Brahim Samba Diouf v Ministre du Travail, de l'Emploi et de l'Immigration*, Judgment of 28 July 2011, Unreported.

concerned an application for international protection (specifically asylum) submitted by a Mauritanian citizen, which was rejected in the course of an accelerated procedure on the ground that he had produced a forged passport and could not substantiate the risk for being killed or forced into slavery. In addition, his fears of reprisal by his employer were found not to amount to persecution under the Geneva Convention as there was no political, ethnic or religious background to the case. In this case the ECJ was asked whether the Asylum Procedures Directive or the general principle of effective remedy under EU law as entrenched in Articles 6 and 13 ECHR, required an appeal against an administrative authority's decision on granting international protection made in the context of accelerated procedures. AG Cruz Villalon found that Article 47 of the EU Charter provided more extensive protection than the ECHR.[77] In the Court's view, the conformity of the Asylum Procedures Directive was to be evaluated with regard to Article 47 of the EU Charter and 'therefore, *indirectly*, with the minimum content of the right to an effective remedy as represented by the requirements of the European Convention on Human Rights.'[78] It was held that the lack of appeal proceedings against accelerated administrative proceedings is not precluded under EU law on the condition that the reasons which led to the decision to apply this procedure can be subject to judicial review. According to Ippolito what is puzzling is that despite similarities with the legal reasoning of the ECtHR's cases, most notably *Jabary*,[79] the Luxembourg Court preferred not to consider the case-law of the Strasbourg Court.[80]

An example of "progressive" interpretation is the *Salahadin Abdulla and Others* case,[81] which is also one of the first asylum cases where reference to the EU Charter as a key human rights instrument was made. The case concerned the revocation by the German authorities of the refugee status of Iraqi nationals as a result of the change in circumstances in Iraq. In particular, the ECJ held that the Qualification Directive provisions 'must be interpreted in a manner which respects the fundamental rights and the principles recognized in particular by the Charter.'[82] Such an

[77] According to AG Cruz Villalon 'the right to effective judicial protection has, through being recognized as part of European Union law by virtue of Article 47, acquired a separate identity and substance under that Article which are not the mere sum of the provisions of Articles 6 and 13 of the ECHR. In other words, once the right to effective judicial protection is recognized and guaranteed by the European Union, that fundamental right goes on to acquire a content of its own. [...] European Union law as a system of law has given rise to the development of its own set of defining principles.' (at para 39).

[78] See *Samba Diouf* at para 34. Emphasis added.

[79] See *Jabari v. Turkey*, Application No 40035/98.

[80] See Ippolito in Ippolito and Velluti (2014), see footnote 26.

[81] See Joined Cases C-175/08, C-176/08, C-178/08 and C-179/08, *Salahadin Abdulla & Others*, ECR [2009] I-1493; see Ref. [30].

[82] See *Abdulla*, at para 54.

approach has been reaffirmed in *Bolbol*[83] and in Joined Cases *Germany v. B. and Germany v. D. and others.*[84] In the former case, the ECJ held that by applying the Qualification Directive in accordance with the EU Charter only those persons who have actually availed themselves of the United Nations Relief and Works Agency for Palestine Refugees in the Near East (UNRWA)'s assistance come within the exclusion clause in Article 12(1)(a). In so doing, it adopted an interpretation of Article 12(1)(a) of the Qualification Directive which reproduced Article 1D of the 1951 Geneva Convention. It excluded, therefore, from the scope of the Qualification Directive persons receiving protection or assistance from bodies or agencies of the United Nations. On the basis of this more generous interpretation, therefore, Ms Bolbol who was a stateless person of Palestinian origin from the Gaza Strip who sought asylum in Hungary and who did not avail herself of protection or assistance from UNRWA prior to her application for refugee status, was able to have her case examined on an individual basis under Article 2(c) of the Qualification Directive. The ECJ agreed with the line of thinking of AG Sharpston who disagreed with the interpretation of Article 1D put forward by the Office of the UNHCR.[85]

In *B and D*, the ECJ again interpreted the Qualification Directive in the light of the EU Charter and held that a former member of a terrorist group is not automatically excluded from the status of refugee. In particular, it held that the decision whether to grant refugee status is conditional on an individual assessment of the specific facts making it possible to determine whether there are serious reasons for considering that in the context of his activities within that organization, the person concerned can be held personally responsible for acts of terrorism. Such an individual assessment of responsibility has to be made in the light of both objective and subjective criteria.[86] To that end, according to the Court the following considerations should be taken into account: the effective role of the asylum-seeker in the perpetration of the acts, his/her position within the organization, the extent of the knowledge he/she had or should have had about the activity of the group, any pressure to which he/she was exposed, or other factors likely to have influenced his/her conduct.[87] Further, Member States may not exclude him/her from the refugee status except if he/she has committed a crime of exceptional seriousness.[88]

NS and ME was the ECJ's "response" to the *MSS* ruling by the ECtHR. It concerned Afghan, Iranian and Algerian asylum-seekers who challenged their return from the United Kingdom and Ireland to Greece under the Dublin

---

[83] See Case C-31/09, *Bolbol v Bevandorlasi es Allampolgarsagi Hivatal* ECR [2010] I-5539; see Ref. [31].

[84] See Joined Cases C-57/09 and C-101/09, *Germany v. B. and Germany v. D. and others*, Unreported 17 June 2010, and Opinion of AG Mengozzi, 1 June 2010, at para 78.

[85] See Case C-31/09 *Bolbol* Opinion of AG Sharpston 4 March 2010, at para 38.

[86] See *Germany v B and Germany v D*, at paras. 94 and 96.

[87] Ibidem, at para 97.

[88] Ibidem, at para 108.

Regulation.[89] The judgment makes it clear that a Member State may potentially infringe Article 4 of the EU Charter if it transfers an asylum-seeker to another Member State in certain circumstances. The decision is also important in clarifying the applicability of the EU Charter to the United Kingdom and Poland according to Protocol 30. In particular, it was held that Article 1(1) of Protocol 30 merely "explains" Article 51 of the EU Charter and is not a provision which amounts to an opt-out. However, as noted by Mellon neither the Grand Chamber nor the Advocate General considered in much detail the more contentious issue of the applicability of Title IV (on 'Solidarity') concerning social and economic rights, where Article 1(2) of Protocol 30 is likely to have more effect.[90]

AG Trstenjak[91] opined that if there is a serious risk that the fundamental rights under the EU Charter of the asylum-seeker to be transferred may be breached in the Member State having primary responsibility, the other Member States may not transfer an asylum-seeker to that Member State. Rather, the other Member States are, in principle, obliged to exercise the right to assume responsibility under Article 3(2) of the Dublin Regulation and must themselves examine the asylum application. As regards the question of whether the protection afforded by the rights set out in Articles 1, 18 and 47 of the EU Charter was wider than that afforded by Article 3 ECHR, the Advocate-General stated somewhat cautiously that under Article 52(3) of the EU Charter it must be ensured that the protection guaranteed by the Charter in the areas in which the provisions of the EU Charter overlap with the provisions of the ECHR is no less than the protection granted by the ECHR[92] and that 'particular significance and high importance' had to be attached to the ECtHR case-law in connection with the interpretation of the relevant provisions of the EU Charter by the ECJ.[93] On this "silence" Costello notes that the question had lost salience since the *MSS* ruling where transfers to Greece were held to be in breach of Article 3 ECHR. At the time of *KRS*[94] the question could have been of some relevance because in the absence of an Article 3 ECHR engagement the focus of attention would have moved to Article 4 of the EU Charter, namely, whether removal could amount to a breach of the EU Charter.[95]

Similarly, the Court did not enter into the merit of whether the right to asylum under Article 18 of the EU Charter overlaps with Articles 1 and 47, as well as Articles 4 and 19(2). In addition, the ECJ also stated that the judgments of the ECtHR 'essentially always constitute case-specific judicial decisions and not rules

---

[89] See Joined cases C-411/10 and C-493/10, *N. S. v Secretary of State for the Home Department et M. E. and Others v Refugee Applications Commissioner and Minister for Justice, Equality and Law Reform*, Judgment of Unreported; for case comment and critical analysis, see Refs. [32–34].

[90] See Mellon, see footnote 89, at 661.

[91] See *NS and ME*, Opinion of AG Trstenjak, of 22 September 2011.

[92] See *NS and ME*, Opinion of AG Trstenjak, at para 148.

[93] See *NS and ME*, Opinion of AG Trstenjak, at para 146.

[94] See Application No. 32733/08.

[95] See Costello (2012), see footnote 11, at 327.

of the ECHR themselves, and it would therefore be wrong to regard the case-law of the European Court of Human Rights as a source of interpretation with full validity in connection with the application of the Charter.'[96] By the same token, the ECJ also remained silent on the scope of the right to asylum in Article 18 of the EU Charter.[97] Instead, it merely upheld the need to exercise the sovereignty clause and, in particular, it held the responsibility of the sending state under Article 3(2) Dublin Regulation for the asylum's application when there are 'systemic deficiencies in the asylum procedure and reception conditions for asylum applicants' resulting in inhuman or degrading treatment, within the meaning of Article 4 of the EU Charter.[98] The extent to which breaches of other EU fundamental rights should prevent transfer remains to be seen. In contrast to the Opinion of the Advocate General, the ECJ decided to focus on Article 4 of the EU Charter probably in consideration of the fact that, given the inclusion therein of important fundamental social rights, including other breaches could have opened the floor to different non-*refoulement* claims.[99] The Court clarified that the EU asylum system cannot operate on the basis of a 'conclusive presumption' that all EU Member States 'observe the fundamental rights of the European Union.'[100] Moreover, the ECJ referred to 'the extent of the infringement of fundamental rights described in *MSS v. Belgium and Greece*[101] and, in particular, the absence of any guarantee that the asylum application would be seriously examined by the Greek authorities and the exposure of the applicant to conditions of detention and living conditions that amounted to degrading treatment,'[102] to determine that the existence of "systemic deficiencies" in the asylum procedure and reception conditions for asylum applicants resulting in inhuman or degrading treatment form a basis for rebuttal of the presumption of equivalent protection.

However, in defining the burden of proof test to rebut the presumption of safety according to which a Member State 'cannot be unaware' of such systemic

---

[96] See *NS and ME*, Opinion of AG Trstenjak, at para 146.

[97] On the content of the right to asylum in Article 18 of the EU Charter and the right to an effective remedy in Article 47 of the EU Charter, see UNHCR (2011), UNHCR Oral Submissions in Joined Cases of NS (C-411/10) and ME and Others (C-493/10) Hearing of the Court of Justice of the EU Luxembourg, 28 June 2011 available at: http://www.refworld.org/pdfid/4e1b10bc2.pdf. The Court did not use either the indicators for the determination of the breach's seriousness developed by the UNHCR in its oral submission or the points on the impact of the breach on the individual.

[98] See *NS and ME*, at paras 84, 86, 94 and 106. On the contrary, "serious" risks of infringements of individual provisions of the Common European Asylum System Directives in the Member State primarily responsible are not sufficient to create an obligation on the part of the transferring state to assume responsibility for the asylum examination, provided these infringements do not also violate the Charter rights of the asylum-seeker to be transferred. This mirror's the Opinion of the Adovate general (at para 127).

[99] On this point, see Costello (2012), see footnote 11, at 332.

[100] See *NS and ME*, at para 105.

[101] See Application No. 30696/09.

[102] See *N.S. and M.E.*, at paras 86 and 94.

deficiencies, it did not refer to the part of the *MSS* judgment where the ECtHR, in consideration of the inherent vulnerability of asylum-seekers as a group, developed the concept of a "shared burden of proof."[103] Similarly, it did not refer to *MSS* when it argued that a country may gather information from the reports of international organizations, the UNHCR[104] as well the European Commission, which were the same mentioned by the ECtHR.[105] Likewise, in relation to the standard of proof the ECJ relied on its own autonomous interpretation of "serious risk" and did not refer to the concept of "substantial grounds for a real risk" developed by the ECtHR.[106] According to the Meijers Committee, in relation to assessing whether the national authorities of the sending State "knew or ought to have known" about the risk of ill-treatment in the country of destination, Member States should be obliged to report on the length of the procedure, the detention conditions and reception capacity in relation to the inflow of asylum-seekers to EASO and the Commission statistical data (the Asylum Management Reporting System), on a quarterly basis.[107] Hence, what transpires from the foregoing analysis of *NS and ME* is that both the ECJ and the Advocate General are emphasizing the importance of the EU Charter's provisions and the autonomy of the EU legal order whilst at the same time being mindfully respectful of the ECHR and the case-law of the ECtHR.

The foregoing predilection for an autonomous interpretation of EU law and the EU Charter provisions does not only concern those cases where the content of the right in the EU legal order and in the ECHR differs. Even in cases where the content of the right may be considered identical the ECJ seems to be reluctant to rely on the ECtHR case law. *Y and Z*[108] seems to confirm this proposition. The referring court asked whether and, if so, to what extent an act restricting freedom

---

103 See *MSS*, at paras 352 and 359. This was in line with the position of UNCAT, see *Agiza v. Sweden* (2005, at para 13.7); *A.S. v. Sweden* (2000, at para 8.6) and with the view of the UN Sub-Commission for the Promotion of Human Rights, namely that once a *general* risk situation is established, there is a 'presumption' that the person would face a real risk, see UN Sub-Commission on the Promotion and Protection of Human Rights (2005), Resolution 2005/12 on Transfer of Persons, 10 Aug. 2005, at para 4.

104 In *MSS* the Grand Chamber of the European Court of Human Rights (ECtHR) attached "critical importance" to UNHCR's views, see *MSS* at para 349.

105 In *MSS*, the ECtHR mentioned the European Commission's infringement procedures against Greece, in 2006 and 2008, regarding the country's failure to apply the Reception Conditions Directive and to comply with its obligations under the Dublin Regulation by not adopting the laws, regulations and administrative measures necessary to ensure the examination of applications by asylum-seekers transferred back to Greece under the terms of the Regulation.

106 This concept was first developed by the ECtHR outside EU asylum cases (see e.g. *Soering v. United Kingdom*, Application No. 14038/88) and has subsequently been applied to Dublin returns (see e.g. *T.I. v. United Kingdom*, Application No. 43844/98, *K.R.S. v. United Kingdom*, Application No. 32733/08 and *MSS*, Application No. 30696/09.

107 See Ref. [35].

108 See Joined Cases C-71/11 and C-99/11 *Federal Republic of Germany v Y and Z* Judgment of the Court (Grand Chamber) of 5 September 2012, nyr.

of religion and, in particular, the universal right of freedom of worship, constitutes an "act of persecution" within the meaning of Article 9(1)(a) of the Qualification Directive. Y and Z, were two Pakistani nationals, members of the Ahmadiyya minority community (a minority not recognized by the Muslim majority) who claimed that they were forced to leave Pakistan because of their membership to that community, and who applied for asylum in Germany. The German authorities rejected Y and Z's applications for asylum, finding that the restrictions on the public practice of faith imposed on Ahmadis in Pakistan did not constitute persecution for the purposes of the right of asylum. In his Opinion AG Bot[109] proposed an interpretation which followed the ECtHR's jurisprudence.[110] In particular, 'a severe violation of freedom of religion, regardless of which component of that freedom is targeted by the violation, is likely to amount to an "act of persecution" where the asylum-seeker, by exercising that freedom or infringing the restrictions placed on the exercise of that freedom in his country of origin, runs a real risk of being executed or subjected to torture, or inhuman or degrading treatment, of being reduced to slavery or servitude or of being prosecuted or imprisoned arbitrarily.'[111]

The Court, unlike the Advocate General, was more laconic and stated that it might be the case 'where an applicant for asylum, as a result of exercising that freedom in his country of origin, runs a genuine risk of, *inter alia*, being prosecuted or subject to inhuman or degrading treatment or punishment by one of the actors referred to in Article 6 of the Directive.'[112] In particular, no reference was made to the ECtHR' decision in *Z and T v United Kingdom.*[113] This is quite surprising if we consider that not only freedom of religion is guaranteed in the same terms in both the EU Charter and in the ECHR but also that the question submitted to the ECtHR was very similar to the one submitted to the Luxembourg Court by the German referring court. In spite of the lack of reference to the ECtHR's judgment, the decision of the ECJ is a welcomed development. According to the ECJ, it is not the public or private, or collective or individual nature of the manifestation and practice of the religion which will determine whether a violation of the right to freedom of religion should be regarded as persecution, but the severity of the measures and sanctions adopted or liable to be adopted against the person concerned.[114] In that context, the Court held that a violation of the right to freedom of religion may constitute persecution where, because of the exercise of that liberty in his country of origin, there is a genuine risk that the asylum applicant will, *inter alia*, be prosecuted or subject to inhumane

---

[109] See Joined Cases C-71/11 and C-99/11, *Federal Republic of Germany v Y and Z*, Judgment of the Court (Grand Chamber) of 5 September 2012, Unreported, Opinion of AG Bot, 23 April 2012.

[110] See *Z* and *T v United Kingdom*, Application No. 27034/05, 28 February 2006.

[111] Ibidem, at para 86.

[112] See *Y and Z,* at para 67.

[113] See Application No. 27034/05.

[114] See *Y and Z,* at paras. 58–66.

or degrading punishment.[115] In the light of this, the Court held that, where it is established that, upon his return to his country of origin, the person concerned will engage in a religious practice which will expose him to a real risk of persecution, he should be granted refugee status.[116]

In *K*,[117] concerning a woman who entered Poland irregularly, applied for asylum and then without awaiting the decision moved to Austria irregularly to rejoin one of her adult sons who was already a refugee in that country, the ECJ was asked to clarify on the application of the humanitarian clause in Article 15 and sovereignty clause in Article 3 of the Dublin Regulation. The ECJ again declined to clarify whether Article 18 of the EU Charter amounted to a free-standing right to asylum. That said, it affirmed that the objective of the Dublin Regulation must be to ensure effective access of the asylum-seeker to refugee status determination.[118]

With regard to the questions made by the referring court, the ECJ declined to consider the issue of whether the sovereignty clause may be applied beyond the risk of an infringement of Article 4 of the EU Charter and whether a more extensive notion of "inhuman treatment" or "family" (differing from that of the ECtHR) may be applied.[119] Nevertheless, the overall outcome of the decision is a positive one as ultimately it promotes the importance of family unification also for refugees.[120] The Court adopted a teleological reading of the humanitarian clause in Article 15 of the Dublin Regulation and in so doing it transformed the discretion to promote family unity contained in the "humanitarian clause" into an automatic obligation.[121] In this respect, it may be posited that it goes beyond *NS and ME* as in that case the Court, in contrast to the Advocate General, refused to maintain that a Member State had a duty to take responsibility for the asylum-seeker if a Dublin transfer would expose them to serious risk of violating fundamental rights.

In *Halaf*,[122] a Dublin transfer case concerning an Iraqi national who had unsuccessfully applied for asylum in Bulgaria, the ECJ was asked, *inter alia*, what the content of the right to asylum under Article 18 of the EU Charter is in conjunction with Article 53 of the EU Charter and in conjunction with the definition in Article 2(c) and Recital 12 of the Dublin II Regulation. Hence, the ECJ was asked (again) to clarify whether Article 18 of the EU Charter amounts to a free-standing right to asylum and whether a breach of such a right in cases of a

[115] Ibidem, at paras 68–71.

[116] Ibidem, at para 79.

[117] See Case C-245/11, *K v Bundesasylamt*, Judgment of the Court (Grand Chamber) of 6 November 2012, nyr.

[118] Ibidem, at para 48.

[119] Ibidem, at para 55.

[120] Ibidem, at para 52.

[121] Ibidem, at para 53.

[122] See Case C-528/11, *Zuheyr Frayeh Halaf v Darzhavna agentsia za bezhantsite pri Ministerskia savet*, nyr, Judgment of 30 May 2013.

transfer would not be avoided. Regrettably, the Court deviated from answering the question by rephrasing the question of the referring court and arguing that the latter was based on the incorrect assumption that a Member State may examine an application for asylum on the basis of the sovereignty clause only if it is shown that the Member State responsible under the Dublin Regulation would not respect the right to asylum *as per* Article 18 of the EU Charter. The Court then, in a rather perfunctory manner, simply stated that because the option under Article 3(2) of the Dublin Regulation is not subject to any particular condition there is no need to answer the question concerning the content of the right to asylum in Article 18 of the EU Charter.[123]

In the *Puid* case,[124] concerning an Iranian national who applied for asylum in Germany, the key question is whether an asylum-seeker may be said to have a personal enforceable right against a Member State deriving from Article 3(2) of the Dublin Regulation. In particular, the question posed by the national referring court is whether a duty of the Member States to exercise the sovereignty clause under Article 3(2) Dublin Regulation can also be inferred from reasons not directly associated with the asylum-seeker himself or other particularities of an individual case, but which result from a legal or administrative situation in the Member State assuming responsibility that pose a threat to the fundamental rights of asylum-seekers under the EU Charter. As already seen above, in *MSS* the ECtHR, in assessing the risk of ill-treatment in the Member State responsible according to the criteria set out in the Dublin Regulation, took into consideration the general country's situation in order to establish the risk of ill-treatment, rather than the individual circumstances of the asylum-seeker.

In his Opinion, AG Jääskinen maintains that asylum-seekers do not have an enforceable claim to compel a Member State to examine their applications for asylum in accordance with the Article 3(2) of the Dublin Regulation as the latter has not been conceived to vest individuals with rights but rather in organizing relationships between Member States.[125] However, the Advocate General, following the decision in *NS and ME*[126] opines that in "exceptional situations," namely, those that fulfil both the substantive and the evidential threshold set out by the Court in *NS and ME,* a national court that cannot be unaware that systemic deficiencies in the asylum procedure and in the reception conditions of asylum-seekers in the Member State responsible under the Dublin Regulation amount to substantial grounds for believing that, asylum-seekers would face a real risk of being subjected to inhuman or degrading treatment within the meaning of Article 4 of the EU Charter, is obliged to suspend the transfer of asylum-seekers to that

[123] See *Halaf*, at paras 40–42.

[124] See Case C-4/11, *Federal Republic of Germany v Kaveh Puid* pending, OJ C 95/3-4, 26 March 2011.

[125] See *Puid* Opinion of AG Jääskinen, 18 April 2013 at paras 57–58.

[126] Ibidem, at paras 3 and 39–45.

Member State.[127] More specifically, the competent authorities have a positive obligation to desist from transferring asylum applicants to the responsible Member State *proprio motu* so as not to expose an asylum-seeker to inhuman and degrading treatment, prohibited by Article 4 of the EU Charter. In this context, the Advocate General also seems to be preoccupied with the effects that such a rationale, as developed in *NS and ME*, may have on the principle of mutual trust. He thus goes on to clarify that 'the Court has aimed at establishing a high barrier against the setting aside of the principle of mutual trust underlying Regulation No. 343/2003. This means that *the principle of mutual trust may not be placed under question through systematic examination*, in each procedure entailing an application for asylum.'[128] What transpires from the Opinion is the primacy of the principle of non-*refoulement* and its absolute nature. However, this is done by emphasizing that the circumstances such as the one in the present case are "exceptional situations" and also by heralding the importance of the principle of mutual trust in the Dublin system. In the Opinion there is no reference to the ECHR and the ECtHR's case-law and the Advocate General, therefore, seems to be following a series of cases of the ECJ which favour an autonomous interpretative approach.

With regard to detention, the key case is *Kadzoev,*[129] a case concerning the limitation of pre-deportation detention of asylum-seekers. This was the first judgment on the Returns Directive. The case was about an applicant of Chechen origin, Kadzoev, who applied for asylum in Bulgaria. The Bulgarian authorities rejected his application and ordered his expulsion as an illegal immigrant. However, his expulsion to Russia was not possible, as he had no identity documents issued by the Russian authorities. Pending a solution allowing his return to Russia or to another third country, Kadzoev was detained in a detention centre for more than 3 years. Under the PPU procedure, the ECJ was asked to clarify the scope of Article 15 of Returns Directive,[130] with a particular emphasis on the obligation for Member States not to exceed the maximum period of 18 months pursuant to paragraphs 5 and 6 of the same provision. The reasoning of the ECJ and the Advocate General were similar, although the Opinion provided much more detailed analysis. AG Mazák grounded his reasoning in the 'reasonable prospect of removal' under Article 15(4) of the Returns Directive on the basis that EU law also incorporated the Article 5(1)(f) ECHR standards. In so doing, the Advocate General cited *Chalal* and chiefly

---

[127] Ibidem, at paras 61 and 63.

[128] Ibidem, at para 62. Emphasis added.

[129] See Case C-357/09 PPU, *Said Shamilovich Kadzoev*, [2009] ECR I-11189; there is also a case pending before the ECtHR concerning the lawfulness of his detention under the ECHR, see *Kadzoev v Bulgaria*, Application No. 56437/07, introduced on 20 December 2007.

[130] See European Parliament and Council of the European Union (2008) Directive 2008/115/EC of the European Parliament and of the Council of 16 December 2008 on common standards and procedures in Member States for returning illegally staying third-country nationals, OJ L 348/98, 24.12.2008.

Mikolenko[131] according to which detention was unlawful as there was no reasonable prospect of removal due to insufficient cooperation from the receiving country. Significantly, the Advocate General referred to the Council of Europe documents, particularly the CAHAR Guideline Number Seven on Forced Return.[132] At the same time, *Kadzoev* also suggests that the standards of protection afforded by the Returns Directive are higher than those provided by the ECHR particularly in relation to the requirement that detention is necessary to ensure removal.[133]

Similarly, in *El Dridi*[134] the Court observed that the Returns Directive took into account both the case-law of the ECtHR[135] and CAHAR Guideline No. 8., both on the limitation of duration of pre-deportation detention.[136]

These two detention cases illustrate the interactions between the two European Courts. However, important differences remain in terms of the level of protection afforded. As seen above,[137] the ECtHR rejects the requirements of necessity and proportionality in its case law, using "reasonable time" as the benchmark for assessing arbitrariness. As Costello points out, 'it would be regrettable if the distinctive EU version of proportionality were to be sapped of vigor by converging on the weak ECHR non-arbitrariness standard.'[138] For Cornelisse the likelihood of this occurring is improbable in consideration of the fact that Member States, when implementing EU law, are bound by the EU Charter, which permits limitations on the right to personal liberty only if these are proportionate and necessary, and genuinely meet objectives of general interest that are recognized by the Union.[139]

4.4 Reflecting on the Role of the European Courts in the Protection of Asylum-Seekers' Human Rights

The findings of the previous section show that the adoption of the EU Charter, particularly since it acquired the same legal value as the EU Treaties,[140] has had and is having a significant impact on the development of CEAS. In particular,

---

[131] See *Chahal v. United Kingdom*, Application No.22414/93, 23; *Mikolenko v. Estonia*, Application No. 10664/05.

[132] See Council of Europe (2005), '*Ad hoc* Committee of Experts on the Legal Aspects of Territorial Asylum, Refugees and Stateless Persons (CAHAR)—Twenty Guidelines on forced return' available at: https://wcd.coe.int/ViewDoc.jsp?id=858071&Site=COE.

[133] See *Kadzoev*, at para 64.

[134] See Case C-61/11 PPU *Hassen El Dridi alias Soufi Karim*, Judgment of the Court (First Chamber) of 28 April 2011, nyr.

[135] In particular it cited *Saadi*, Application No. 13229/03.

[136] See Council of Europe (2005), footnote see footnote 131.

[137] See above, Sect. 4.2.

[138] See Costello (2012), see footnote 177 in Chap. 3, at 302.

[139] See Cornelisse, see footnote 95 in Chap. 2, at p. 221.

[140] See Article 6(1) TEU.

through a series of key cases of the ECJ the EU Charter is being brought to life and is rapidly becoming a vital hermeneutic tool for the Luxembourg Court in order to substantiate and shape the actual content and scope of basic human rights for asylum-seekers, contained in a rather inchoate manner in key EU asylum legislative instruments. The ECJ's judicial activism combined with the equally important "monitoring" function of the ECtHR is filling in the *lacunae* of EU asylum legislation, which in spite of the recast process remain.

In turn, in the context of a changing juridical landscape, these judicial developments beg the question of what type of relationship there is between the ECJ and the ECtHR. Is it one wrought with conflict, destined to deteriorate and peril? With EU accession to the European Convention looming large on the horizon, this view clearly does not have any solid foundation. Nor is it one of passionate love though, as seen in the foregoing jurisprudential analysis. The answer is most plausibly somewhere in-between.

Since the EU Charter entered the scene, the reference made to the ECHR and the ECtHR' case law appears to be mostly confirmatory of a fundamental right or principle, determined through an *autonomous* interpretation of EU law. In particular, this has been the case when according to the ECJ the content of the right in the EU legal order did not "match" in its entirety that of the corresponding right contained in the ECHR. However, at the same time, both the Court and the Advocate General have adopted a respectful and mindful approach to the ECHR and the Strasbourg Court's case-law.

Still, is the emphasis placed on interpretative autonomy and/or distinctiveness of the EU legal order by the ECJ problematic from the perspective of asylum-seekers' effective human rights' protection? Or, to put it differently, does the focus on autonomy (and a concern for its preservation) on the part of the ECJ and, linked to this, the emergence of what may be coined as "parallel human rights legal regimes,"[141] lead to an incoherent and patchy framework of human rights' protection? Incoherence has potentially negative effects on the protection of asylum-seekers' human rights[142] and it is thus a legitimate concern. However, there are strong reasons—both legal and of a more pragmatic nature-suggesting otherwise. First, Article 52(3) of the EU Charter regulates the relationship between the two European human rights systems by tying to the EU Charter the meaning and scope of those rights which correspond to the rights of the European Convention. While no reference to the case law of the ECtHR is to be found in the provisions of the EU Charter, the Explanations to Article 52(3) clearly state that 'paragraph 3 is intended to ensure the necessary consistency between the Charter and the ECHR'

[141] Garlicki talks about "multidimensionality of constitutional protection of human rights" to refer to the growing phenomenon of overlapping legal regimes for the international protection of asylum-seekers and refugees, see Ref.[36], at 509; see also Costello who in relation to detention illustrates how different human rights bodies 'speak with different voices […], a phenomenon that is […] explained by their different institutional contexts and decisional autonomy', see Costello (2012), see footnote 177 in Chap. 3, at 260.

[142] On the consequences of incoherence, see further Ref. [37].

and 'the scope of the guaranteed rights are determined also by the case-law of the ECJ and the ECtHR.[143] Both the EU Charter and the European Convention contain a general non-regression clause as a further safeguard.[144] Moreover, Article 52(7) clearly states that 'the Explanations shall be given due regard by the courts of the Union and of the Member States.' In addition, we have already seen that the Luxembourg and Strasbourg Courts have often opted for some kind of diplomacy, relying on an informal platform to resolve any collision or conflict and generally mutually acknowledging each other's jurisdiction.[145]

Hence, it may be argued that in relation to asylum-seekers' human rights the role of the European Courts remains key to ensuring their effective protection, particularly in the light of a lack of real progress following the reform of EU asylum law. What seems 'to emerge is a shared view and understanding that human rights should be better protected through the development of a "European" *ius commune* and that a certain optimization of "judicial cooperation" may contribute to this aim.'[146] Arguably, more than "a parallel interpretation" of the EU Charter and the ECHR might be taking place, albeit at an embryonic stage: a 'kind of bilateral interplay between the EU and Convention law, thereby producing a twofold process of "conventionalization" of Union law and "unionization" of Convention law, though with different timings and intensities.'[147]

References

1. Ripoll Servent A, Trauner F (2012) Do supranational institutions make a difference? EU asylum before and after communitarization. Paper presented at the UACES 42nd annual conference exchanging ideas on Europe 2012 old borders-new frontiers, Passau, Germany, 3–5 Sept 2012
2. Jacobs F (2007) The sovereignty of law: the European way—the hamlyn lectures 2006. Cambridge University Press, Cambridge
3. Lawson RA (2009) Ex Boreale Lux—on the influence of the ECJ on the interpretation of the ECHR. In: Bulterman MK, Hancher LR, McDonnell AM, Sevenster HG (eds) Views of European law from the mountain—liber amicorum for Piet Jan Slot. The Hague, Kluwer, pp 439–454
4. Lawson RA (1994) Confusion or conflict? diverging interpretations of the European convention on human rights in strasbourg and luxembourg. In: Lawson RA, de Blois M (eds) The dynamics of the protection of human rights in Europe. Essays in honour of Henry G. Schermers, (Dorderecht: Martinus Nijhoff Publishers), vol 3, pp 219–252

[143] See Praesidium of the European Convention (2007), see footnote 143 in Chap. 2.

[144] See Article 53 of the EU Charter equivalent to Article 53 ECHR.

[145] See Iglesias Sánchez, see footnote 136 in Chap. 2; see also Scheeck (2005), see footnote 5 and Scheeck (2009), see footnote 7.

[146] See Ippolito in Ippolito and Velluti (2014), see footnote 26; on the concept of a "European ius commune", see Ref. [40].

[147] See J. Callewaert (2008), see footnote 62, at p. 114.

5. Douglas-Scott S (2006) A tale of two courts: luxembourg. Strasbourg and the growing European human rights acquis, common market law review 43:619–655
6. Spielman D (1999) Human rights case law in the strasbourg and luxembourg courts: inconsistencies and complementarities. In: Alston P, Heenan J, Bustelo M (eds) The EU and human rights. Oxford University Press, Oxford, pp 757–780
7. Scheeck L (2005) The relationship between the European courts and integration through human rights, Heidelberg. J Intern Law 65:837–885
8. Costa JP, Skouris (2011), Joint communication from Presidents Costa and Skouris of 24 January 2011. Available at:http://www.echr.coe.int/NR/rdonlyres/02164A4C-0B63-44C3-80C7-FC594EE16297/0/2011Communication_CEDHCJUE_EN.pdf
9. Scheeck L (2009) The diplomacy of European judicial networks in times of constitutional crisis. In: Snyder F, Maher I (eds) The evolution of the European Courts: change and continuity. Bruylant, Brussels, pp 17–36
10. Costello C (2012) Courting access to asylum in Europe: recent supranational jurisprudence explored. Hum Rights Law Rev 12(2):287–339
11. den Heijer M (2008) Whose rights and which rights? the continuing story of non-refoulement under the European convention on human rights. Eur J Migr Law 10(3):277–314
12. Mole N, Meredith C (2010) Asylum and the European convention on human rights. Council of Europe, Strasbourg
13. Spijkerboer T (2009) Subsidiarity and arguability: the European court of human rights, case law on judicial review in asylum cases. Int J Refugee Law 21(1):48–74
14. Lock T (2011) Walking on a tightrope: the draft accession agreement and the autonomy of the EU legal order. Common Mark Law Rev 48:1025–1054
15. Lock T (2010) EU accession to the ECHR: implications for the judicial review in Strasbourg. Eur Law Rev 35(6):777–798
16. Meara NO (2011) A more secure europe of rights? The European court of human rights, the court of justice of the European union and EU accession to the ECHR. Ger Law J 12(10):1813–1832
17. Van de Heyning C, Lawson R (2011) The EU as a party to the European convention of human rights: EU law and the European court of justice case law as inspiration and challenge to the European court of human rights jurisprudence. In: Popelier P, Van De Heyning C, Van Nuffel P (eds) Law and cosmopolitan values, vol 1. Intersentia, Cambridge, pp 35–64
18. Steering Committee for Human Rights (CDDH) (2002) Study of the technical and legal issues of a possible EC/EU accession to the European convention on human rights. In: Report adopted by CDDH at its 53rd meeting, DG-II(2002)006 (CDDH(2002)010 Addendum 2), 25–28 June 2002
19. Clayton G (2011) Asylum-seekers in Europe: MSS v Belgium and Greece. Hum Rights Law Rev 11(4):758–773P
20. Mallia (2011) Case of MSS v. Belgium and Greece: a catalyst in the re-thinking of the Dublin II Regulation. Refug Surv Quart 30(3): 107–128
21. Moreno-Lax V (2012) Dismantling the dublin system: MSS v Belgium and Greece. Eur J Migr Law 14(1):1–31
22. Clayton G (2011) Asylum-seekers in Europe: MSS v Belgium and Greece. Hum Right Law Rev 11(4):758–773
23. Moreno-Lax V (2012) Hirsi Jamaa and others v Italy or the strasbourg court versus extraterritorial migration control? Hum Right Law Rev 12(3):574–598
24. Council of Europe (2010) Report of the parliamentary assembly on the detention of Asylum-Seekers and irregular migrants in Europe. In: Committee on migration, refugees and population Doc.12105, 11 Jan 2010. Available at: http://assembly.coe.int/ASP/Doc/XrefViewHTML.asp?FileID=12435&Language=EN
25. Callewaert J (2008) Unionisation and conventionalisation of fundamental rights in Europe. In: Wouters J, Nollkaemper A, De Wet E (eds) The Europeanisation of public international law: the Status of Public International Law in the EU and its member states. T.M.C Asser Press, BD Den Haag, pp 109–136

26. Carrera S, De Somer M, Petkova B (2012) The court of justice of the European union as a fundamental rights tribunal. In: Challenges for the effective delivery of fundamental rights in the area of freedom, security and justice CEPS. Papers in Liberty and Security, No. 49/August 2012
27. Douglas-Scott S (2006) A tale of two courts: luxembourg, strasbourg and the growing European human rights acquis. Common Market Law Rev 43:629–665
28. Weiss W (2011) Human rights in the EU: rethinking the role of the European convention on human rights after Lisbon. Eur Const Law Rev 7(1):64–95
29. Errera R (2011) The CJEU and subsidiary protection: reflections on elgafaji- and after. Int J Refug Law 23(1):93–112
30. Herrera R (2011) Case comment, cessation and assessment of new circumstances: a comment on Abdulla. Int J Refug Law 23(3):521–537
31. Cardwell PJ (2011) Determining refugee status under directive 2004/83: comment on Bolbol (C-31/09). Eur Law Rev 36(1):135–145
32. Buckley J (2012) Case comment on NS v secretary of state for the home department (C-411/10). Eur Human Right Law Rev 2:205–210
33. Costello C (2012) Dublin-case NS/ME: Finally, an end to blind trust across the EU? A&MR 2:83–92
34. Mellon G (2012) The charter of fundamental rights and the dublin convention: an analysis of N.S. v secretary of state for the home department (C-411/10). Eur Publ Law 18(4): 655–664
35. Mejiers Committee (2012) Letter to the European parliament (LIBE committee). In: The recast of the Dublin regulation (2008/0243 COD) and the proposal for a process for early warning, preparedness and management of Asylum crisis. Available at: http://www.statewatch.org/news/2012/mar/meijers-cttee-letter-EP-dublin.pdf
36. Garlicki L (2008) Cooperation of courts: the role of supranational jurisdictions in Europe. Int J Constitutional Law 6(3/4):509–530
37. Van de Heyning C (2012) Coherence and progress in the European protection of human rights: friends or feuds? Paper presented at the research workshop, a Europe of rights: the EU and the ECHR, School of Law, University of Surrey, 8 and 9 June 2012
38. Gragl P (2013) The Accession of theEuropean Union to the European Convention on Human Rights. Oxford: Hart
39. Ippolito and Velluti (2014) The relationshipbetween the European Court of Justice and the European Court of Human Rights: the case ofasylum. In: Dzehtsiarou K, Konstadinides T, Lock T, & O'Meara N (eds) Human Rights Lawin Europe: The Influence, Overlaps and Contradictions of the EU and ECHR, London: Routledge
40. Delmas-Marty M (2002) Towards a Truly Common Law. Europe as aLaboratory for Legal Pluralism, Cambridge: CUP

Chapter 5
CEAS, Asylum-Seekers and EU Human Rights Post-Lisbon: Closing the Gaps in the European Protection Regime

> The art is to translate the rhetoric of human rights protection into a working reality that is commensurate with human dignity, compatible with international obligations and consistent with the rule of law.[1]

Since Tampere, the EU has rapidly and distinctly asserted itself as a major player in the international refugee regime. CEAS concerns many aspects of asylum, which are now covered by a substantial body of EU asylum law. To date, the relationship between EU asylum law and human rights law has nonetheless been tense. Even after the reform of CEAS, EU asylum legislation remains focused primarily on the prevention of abuses of the asylum system, the restriction of secondary movements of asylum-seekers and the efficient determination of asylum applications, rather than being premised on providing an adequate protection of asylum-seekers' human rights. These significant shortcomings of CEAS are also associated with misconceptions of who an asylum-seeker is. Protection-seekers are often regarded as potential economic migrants (and, linked to this, as a threat to the sustainability of Member States' welfare states as well as public order and safety) rather than as persons who may be in need of international protection. In addition, the "embeddedness" of classical understandings of national sovereignty, the security paradigm and, more broadly, the idea of "Fortress Europe," whereby the dismantling of internal borders between Member States has led to a parallel strengthening of the EU external borders, are all factors explaining why progress in fully developing CEAS has been piecemeal to date. In this context, EU asylum law risks becoming instrumental to a restrictive EU immigration policy.

The analysis carried out throughout this volume shows that the EU's asylum *acquis* contains significant protection gaps. It also exposes the level of complexity involved in developing a fairer and more humane CEAS and, more generally, the challenges that lay ahead.[2] As Cornelisse acutely observes 'the concepts of

---

[1] See Ref. [1], at p. 17.

[2] It is here acknowledged that a true CEAS requires comprehensive solutions covering also the external dimension of EU asylum policy and migration management, and which also address the root-causes of migration. This is examined elsewhere; see Velluti (2014) and see footnote 153 in Chap. 3.

S. Velluti, *Reforming the Common European Asylum System - Legislative Developments and Judicial Activism of the European Courts*, SpringerBriefs in Law,
DOI: 10.1007/978-3-642-40267-8_5, © The Author(s) 2014

constitutionalism and citizenship are not (yet) able to deal with violations of human dignity caused by the territoriality of the modern state' because in spite of the fact that they are underpinned by universalistic ideas about human equality and dignity they remain contextualized within the very particularistic framework of the *territorial* state.[3] What is problematic, however, and to a certain degree unexpected, is the fact that even the discourse of human rights, which aspires to be truly universal and has developed outside a purely national context, has been unable to abstain itself from relying on the idea of a state's sovereign territory.[4] In a rather pessimistic vein, Lui maintains that 'the refugee regime is a form of geopolitical humanitarianism that has as its "core business" the preservation of the value of the nation-state form.'[5] Costello[6] shows how the UDHR exemplifies this[7]: the latter, for instance, refers to 'the right to a nationality' but not in the country of residence or of choice; it protects the 'right to freedom of movement and residence' but only 'within the borders of each state;'[8] the 'right to leave any country, including his own, and to return to his country,'[9] but not to enter another; and the 'right to seek asylum' but not to be granted asylum.[10] One would be led to believe that such statist approach would have become obsolete in an age of human rights and yet in the field of asylum it remains "ingrained in stone."[11]

For the EU to build a credible and robust asylum policy in Europe it will need to identify concrete measures and instruments to adequately balance the tension between the international obligations to admit protection-seekers (and to guarantee access to a basic set of human rights) and the sovereign prerogative of the Member States to control access to their territory. For this to be possible, it needs to ensure *in primis* that EU asylum law is firmly grounded in fundamental human rights and values. The missing link between the *lex lata*[12] and *lex ferenda*[13] of the EU asylum regime is human dignity, the primacy of which is recognized in Article 1 of the EU Charter which states that human dignity is inviolable and it must be respected and *protected*[14] and Article 2 TEU where human dignity is included as one of the

---

[3] See Cornelisse (2011), see footnote 94 in Chap. 2, p. 221.

[4] Idem.

[5] See Ref. [2], at para 6; see also, Ref. [3].

[6] See Costello (2012), see footnote 173 in Chap. 3, at 261.

[7] See also the ECHR. E.g. Articles 2 (on freedom of movement) and 3 (on the prohibition of expulsion of nationals) of Protocol No. 4 of the ECHR as amended by Protocol 11.

[8] See Article 13(1) UDHR.

[9] See Article 13(2) UDHR.

[10] See Article 14(1) UDHR.

[11] See Ref. [4].

[12] Latin term meaning 'what the law is.'

[13] Latin term meaning 'what the law ought to be.'

[14] Emphasis added.

values on which the Union is founded.[15] The centrality of human dignity within the system of the EU Charter can be seen also by the place assigned to human dignity, namely Title 1, which provides the normative features of human dignity in a cluster of key prohibitions assigning the concept with 'its particular gravitas and normative significance.'[16] Protecting human dignity encompasses a duty to protect the right to life,[17] the right to physical and mental integrity,[18] the prohibition of torture, inhuman or degrading treatment,[19] and the prohibition of slavery, forced labour and human trafficking.[20] The guarantee of these fundamental rights is at the basis of the principle of non-*refoulement* and their protection is thus vital for asylum-seekers. Significantly, the EU Charter is not limited in its scope of application to Union citizens but also extends to TCNs. Only a few provisions are limited to EU citizens, which are mainly to be found in Title V and even here there are fundamental rights to which everyone is entitled to.[21]

Dupré aptly writes that human dignity as a constitutional foundation is a response to times of inhumanity and it carries the hope that the regime created by the constitution (which is based in dignity) will foster a democracy (comprising the setting up of appropriate human rights and institutional design) in which human beings can lead a meaningful life and shape their personal and political destiny.[22] The core constitutional meaning of dignity, therefore, is the definition and protection of humanity.[23] In a series of asylum cases we have seen that the ECJ has already been called to shape the scope of human dignity. Arguably, in *NS and ME*, the Court following the Opinion of the AG, provided the basis for elaborating a

---

[15] Article 2 TEU further defines the connotations of human dignity by providing that the foundational values of the Union 'are common to the Member States in a society in which pluralism, non-discrimination, tolerance, justice, solidarity and equality between women and men prevail.'

[16] See Ref. [5].

[17] See Article 2 of the EU Charter.

[18] See Article 3 of the EU Charter.

[19] See Article 4 of the EU Charter.

[20] See Article 5 of the EU Charter.

[21] For example, Article 41 of the EU Charter which protects the right to good administration and Article 47 of the EU Charter on the right to an effective remedy and to a fair trial. When referring to the institutions and bodies of the Union it also includes national authorities when they are carrying out EU law (as per Article 51 of the EU Charter). Consequently, asylum-seekers can rely on Articles 41 and 47 of the EU Charter for requesting that his/her claim be dealt with in an impartial and fair manner and within a reasonable period of time. This argument is further buttressed by the fact that asylum law and policy is now clearly within the remit of EU competence. See e.g. Case C–277/11, *M. M. v Minister for Justice, Equality and Law Reform, Ireland, Attorney General,* Judgment of 22 November 2012, where the ECJ held that that the right to be heard as a fundamental right protected under in the EU Charter (Articles 41 and 47) and a general principle of EU law, must be respected where a Member State considers applications for subsidiary protection in a separate procedure from the refugee status determination (which has the effect of excluding the application of the Procedures Directive), at paras 76 and 82–83.

[22] See Ref. [5], see footnote 16, at 324–325.

[23] Ibidem, at 325.

substantive definition of human dignity in the context of asylum[24] and in future cases it may add further substance to it.

The increased role of the ECJ also urges greater mutual engagement between the EU asylum legal system and the ECHR regime in order to ensure what Costello has coined as "constructive human rights pluralism," which 'describes the desirable mode of interaction between human rights regimes, whereby each cultivates a degree of openness to the others, while maintaining its own integrity.'[25] An example of this can be seen in the minority opinion in *Saadi*, which showed that appropriate engagement with the external International human rights law standards would have led to a different result.[26] *MSS* is also illustrative. The ECtHR held that the detention and living conditions in Greece violated Article 3 ECHR on the basis that the legal commitments to provide reception conditions, in particular under the Reception Conditions Directive, combined with asylum-seekers' particular vulnerability, create specific positive obligations under Article 3 ECHR.

Will this increased cross-fertilization be enough to ensure that the EU's own asylum regime is consistent with the protection imperative of international refugee and human rights law, and that these supranational provisions are consistently implemented across the EU? To achieve this, one solution could be EU accession to the Geneva Convention, which is also mentioned in the Stockholm Programme.[27] However, a study conducted on CEAS illustrates problems concerning its feasibility including technical legal problems for its realization.[28]

A proposal here put forward, in a modest and sketchy form, could be the creation of an *ad hoc* EU asylum court to guarantee compliance with the rules of the European asylum system.[29] The creation of such judicial body would be in combination with steps to improve the retrieval of information across the EU, monitoring of Member States' asylum systems as well as practical cooperation between Member States,[30] also via EASO, and aimed at engendering "positive"

---

[24] In particular, AG Trstenjak opined that the duty not to return derived from the positive protective function inherent in Articles 1 and 4 of the EU Charter, see *NS* Opinion at para 112 and *ME* Opinion at para 63.

[25] See Costello (2012), footnote 173 in Chap. 3, at 260.

[26] Ibidem, at 288.

[27] See above, Stockholm Programme, infra Chap. 1.

[28] See Labayle (2010), see footnote 145 in Chap. 2, at pp. 58–59 and pp. 434–446.

[29] The European Commission has itself put forward a proposal for the creation of a "European Authority on Asylum", see European Commission (2008), Communication from the Commission to the European Parliament, the Council, the European Economic and Social Committee and the Committee of the Regions—Action Plan on Asylum. An Integrated Approach to Protection across the EU' COM (2008) 260 final; for other similar proposals, see Ref. [6].

[30] See Article 70 TFEU, which provides a special legal basis for the creation of a new evaluating mechanism 'to facilitate full application of the principle of mutual recognition,' based on peer review between Member States in collaboration with the Commission. Arguably, this article provides the legal basis for setting up an OMC-like process in the field of asylum. This coordination process could be modeled on the UNHCR's Quality Initiatives (QI) projects which aim at

mutual confidence and recognition of decisions between Member States. The absence of an EU mechanism for monitoring human rights is problematic particularly in the light of Article 18 of the EU Charter. Moreover, the FRA does not have a legal mandate to monitor the respect of human rights by the EU and its Member States, but only to provide them with assistance and expertise.[31]

The legal basis for this new judicial body would be Article 257 TFEU, which envisages the establishment of specialized courts, namely, the creation of a third jurisdictional level below the ECJ and the General Court.[32] While it is recognized that this proposal may clash with reality and, in particular, opposition by the majority of the Member States and perhaps also resistance of some NGOs, it would be endowed with a number of merits, which, *inter alia*, would also address the protection gaps present in CEAS. In particular, the creation of an EU asylum court would address the increasing volume of asylum cases and the failure of national courts to decide them promptly. In general terms, it would streamline and systematize the legal and judicial protection of individuals. Linked to this, it would ensure a common understanding of the legal standards required and applicable to asylum. Clearly, in order to meaningfully address the chief problem underlying asylum policy and law, namely, the security paradigm, the establishment of such judicial body would have to be predicated on ideas of shared and cooperative sovereignty. The main judicial function of the EU asylum court would be to give the final decision to grant protection, for example, on an appeal against a decision of a domestic immigration court or tribunal. The decision of such judicial body could then be subject to an appeal on points of law before the ECJ. It remains to be seen whether this proposal will be taken into consideration at European level in the future.

By way of conclusion, this investigation has unravelled the root-causes of CEAS' shortcomings, explaining why it is neither efficient nor fair by critically

(Footnote 30 continued)
improving the quality of asylum decision-making and using as a benchmark the extent of inclusive application of the Geneva Convention in the context of the specific asylum issue concerned, see e.g. the Asylum Systems Quality Assurance and Evaluation Mechanism (AQSEM), set up in Central and Eastern Europe. Further information is available at: http://www.unhcr-centraleurope.org/pdf/what-we-do/ensuring-legal-protection/refugee-status-determination/quality-initiatives-in-europe.html.

[31] See Council of the European Union (2007), Council Regulation (EC) No 168/2007 of 15 February 2007 establishing a European Union Agency for Fundamental Rights, OJ L53/1, 22.2.2007, Article 4.

[32] See Article 257(1) and (3) TFEU, which provides that: 'The European Parliament and the Council, acting in accordance with the ordinary legislative procedure, may establish specialised courts attached to the General Court to hear and determine at first instance certain classes of action or proceeding brought in specific areas. The European Parliament and the Council shall act by means of regulations either on a proposal from the Commission after consultation of the Court of Justice or at the request of the Court of Justice after consultation of the Commission (para 1).

Decisions given by specialised courts may be subject to a right of appeal on points of law only or, when provided for in the regulation establishing the specialised court, a right of appeal also on matters of fact, before the General Court,' (para 3).

examining the latest reform of key EU asylum legislative instruments and a series of cases of the Luxembourg and Strasbourg Courts. This is not to say that there has not been any progress. Since Tampere, much has been achieved; unimaginable less than 30 years ago. There now is a clearly identifiable EU asylum *acquis* and a human rights discourse underlying EU measures. Further to the changes introduced by the ToL, asylum policy sits among the areas of shared competence of the EU, the EU Charter has acquired legally binding status, and the jurisdiction of the ECJ has been expanded. There is also an on-going dialogue, however complex this might be, between the European Courts. The next step, to use the words of Goodwin-Gill, is to 'translate the rhetoric of human rights protection into a working reality' thereby ensuring the effective protection of human dignity's core foundational elements and thus ensuring *in primis* access to asylum via adequate reception conditions and asylum procedures, leading to a dignifying life for protection-seekers in Europe. As things stand, and in the light of the findings of the present study, the way forward seems to be reform *through* the European Courts.

References

1. Goodwin Gill G (2008) Forced migration: refugees rights and security. In: McAdam J (ed) Studies in international law: forced migration, human rights and security. Hart Publishing, Oxford, pp 1–18
2. Lui R (2002) Governing refugees 1919–1945. Borderlands e J 1(1) Available via http://www.borderlands.net.au/vol1no1_2002/lui_governing.html
3. Benhabib S (2004) The rights of others: aliens, residents and citizens. CUP, Cambridge 11
4. Dauvergne C (2004) Sovereignty, migration and the rule of law in global times. Modern Law Rev 67(4):588–615
5. Dupré C (2013) Human Dignity in Europe: a foundational constitutional principl. Eur Public Law 19(2):319–340
6. North AM, Chia J (2008) Towards convergence in the interpretation of the refugee convention: a proposal for the establishment of an international judicial commission for refugees. In: McAdam J (ed) Studies in international law: forced migration, human rights and security. Hart Publishing, Oxford pp 225–262

MIX
Papier aus verantwortungsvollen Quellen
Paper from responsible sources
FSC® C105338

If you have any concerns about our products,
you can contact us on
ProductSafety@springernature.com

In case Publisher is established outside the EU,
the EU authorized representative is:
Springer Nature Customer Service Center GmbH
Europaplatz 3, 69115 Heidelberg, Germany

Printed by Libri Plureos GmbH
in Hamburg, Germany